PRIDE

weldon**owen**

Published in North America in 2020 by
Weldon Owen International
1150 Brickyard Cove Road
Richmond, CA 94801
www.weldonowen.com

First published in the UK 2019 by André Deutsch Limited
a division of the Carlton Publishing Group

Text © Matthew Todd 2019
Design © André Deutsch Limited 2019

ISBN: 978-1-68188-523-0

10 9 8 7 6 5 4 3 2 1

2020 2021 2022 2023

Printed in Malaysia

Editorial: Isabel Wilkinson, Abigail Wilkinson, Ian Cannon, Madeleine Calvi
Design: Russell Knowles, James Pople
Cover: Allister Fein
Picture Manager: Steve Behan
Production: Marion Storz

PRIDE

THE STORY OF THE

LGBTQ

EQUALITY

MOVEMENT

MATTHEW TODD

Contributors:

Travis Alabanza, Bisi Alimi, Georgina Beyer, Jonathan Blake, Deborah Brin,
Maureen Duffy, David Furnish, Nan Goldin, Asifa Lahore,
Paris Lees, Lewis Oakley, Reverend Troy Perry, Darryl Pinckney, Jake Shears,
Judy Shepard, Aloysius Ssali, Will Young

weldon**owen**

CONTENTS

INTRODUCTION

"The absence of the past was a terror."
So wrote Derek Jarman in his 1992 memoir *At Your Own Risk*.

Jarman wanted people to know what it was like to be a gay man in the mid to late twentieth century. He wrote of a time when people couldn't acknowledge their sexuality, of young lovers killing themselves because it wasn't possible for them to live openly as a couple, and of homophobic doctors falsely telling gay men that they were HIV-positive, hoping to make them "see the error of their ways." He railed against the lack of LGBTQ history at the time, saying how much he needed to have access to it himself and the effect that its suppression has on people like us: it leaves us in a void, not able to have a full sense of who we are and where we've been—no lit path to show how we might live our lives.

In writing this book celebrating the 50th anniversary of the Stonewall riots and the movement that followed, and inviting key figures to contribute essays, it became clear to me quite how much there is to celebrate. The change has been profound, and this explosive event was certainly a turning point. The simple story of a group of people who fought back against homophobic repression has passed into mythology: who exactly was there, who threw the first punch, the first stone, who fought hardest—no one can agree or know for sure. But what is in no doubt is that a community of brave, pissed off, and oppressed people said that enough was enough and took action, knowing that if they didn't, then nobody would.

I've been lucky enough to have seen some of the changes that came about in the wake of that event. I joined the huge crowd outside the House of Commons on the night in February 1994 when it voted on the age of consent. I remember attending the first Stonewall Equality Show in 1994, and my amazement at hearing people say nice things about LGBTQ people. For a while I worked in Stonewall's offices in London, when there was just a handful of staff and volunteers. I answered ever-ringing phones and stuffed newsletters into envelopes, sending them to supporters across the country. If someone had told me then that those homophobic laws would be dissolved or that Prince William would sit for the cover of *Attitude* when I was editor and make a statement against homo, bi, and transphobic bullying, becoming the first royal to appear on the cover of a gay magazine and the first to speak out so plainly, I would not have believed them.

When you read through this book, I hope that you too will feel a very strong sense of celebration, joy, and gratitude towards the countless people who have given time, money, and even their lives to get us where we are today. I can't ever thank those people enough. None of us can. But there's another equally important message that I hope this book carries.

At the 2014 annual Attitude Awards, Maureen Duffy received an Icon Award. Duffy is a successful writer who came out in the 1960s, and who went on national television in 1967 to argue for decriminalization for her gay brothers. She is one of the people to whom we owe so much.

When trans activist Paris Lees presented Duffy with the award, the crowd rose to its feet, cheering. This was a gay woman in her 80s, who had grown up when a gay man could be imprisoned and gay or bi women could have their children taken away from them. If I've seen overwhelming changes, she has seen many more—I expected her to practically levitate to the stage. She didn't do that, nor did she bask in the adulation. Instead she warmly thanked us and then issued a solemn warning.

"We mustn't take our eye off the ball. Think of the people in Uganda, in Iran, who can still be executed for being gay, and that Russia is now going back on its own, previously almost liberal, laws. We can never accept that all is well. We've come a long way, thank goodness . . . but don't hang up your boots."

Engaging on social media in the days afterwards, friends expressed their opinion that the clock could not ever be turned back. We've won the argument, they said. The world is more stable now. This was 2014. Five years later, the UK has voted to leave Europe, Donald Trump is the most powerful person in the world, and there is growing support for right-wing, often homophobic, parties across the world.

This is a time to celebrate. But there is a temptation to idolize the participants in the Stonewall riots to the point where we overlook why they fought: not to be celebrated, not to have books written about them or champagne glasses clinked in their names, but because they had no choice. Today it is becoming increasingly clear that nothing in this world is guaranteed. There are still massive inequalities, as mentioned by Duffy and addressed in this book, which require long overdue action. There are also new dangers coming down the track which will affect us all—the destabilization of the world caused by climate change is right up there. Civilization is what protects, or should protect, the vulnerable, including the LGBTQ community—if civilization collapses as a result of climate change, as Sir David Attenborough recently predicted, what then?

If we really want to honor the people who fought at the Stonewall Inn on that unusually hot June night in 1969, then we need to defend those hard-won rights and confront anything that threatens the free and stable societies protecting them.

Those who wish to control others or have an interest in the status quo will tell you that protest never achieves anything. I hope this book assures you that protest can achieve a great deal, and that when people act together they have true power—and that sometimes using that power is absolutely necessary.

A TIME OF REVOLUTION

People like us have always existed. The identities we associate with the modern terms lesbian, gay, bisexual, transgender, and queer may be relatively modern, but ancient art and literature show that homosexual sex and gender nonconforming behavior have occurred throughout history.

It has been suggested that before the influence of Christianity and colonialism the world was a queer utopia, but in fact disapproval of homosexual behavior existed in most cultures, even when that behavior was sometimes tolerated or permitted. For example, many Native American tribes accepted "two-spirit people," a modern term encompassing a wide range of gender and sexual identities. And there is much evidence of gay sex occurring in ancient cultures from across the world. However, even in ancient Greece and Rome, often held up as examples of the enlightened ancient world because of the social acceptance of sexual relationships between older and younger men, it was still controversial. Plato supported homosexual sex in his early writing but condemned them later, writing that many believed it shameful.

Religious doctrine has had a devastating effect on the ability of LGBTQ people to live their lives fully. Today, many of the countries where homosexual behavior is illegal are either Christian African or Islamic nations. An enormous amount of state-sanctioned homophobia across the globe began with Britain's Buggery Act, which was passed by the English parliament in 1533 and spread across territories as the British Empire expanded. In 1861, the penalty for gay sex was reduced from death to imprisonment. Then, in 1885, British member of parliament Henry Labouchère pushed forward the Criminal Law Amendment Act, making any sexual act between men (even in private) punishable with two years' imprisonment. (This law was used to convict Oscar Wilde in 1895.) Historians have discounted the popular belief that Queen Victoria didn't legislate against lesbianism because she couldn't accept it existed, believing instead that Labouchère was not concerned with Sapphic behavior—or didn't want to alert women to its existence!

In the twentieth century, outside of the tiny number of establishments in a small number of countries where gay people could meet openly, most LGBTQ people either denied their nature or existed in an underground world of secrecy and discretion. Some have since said that life pre-legalization was exciting, but for most, life was difficult, often intolerable; something expressed by the title of the first lesbian novel, *The Well of Loneliness* by Radclyffe Hall, published in 1928. In 1930, the British police set up a special department to catch anyone indulging in "gross indecency." Thousands were imprisoned. In the US, homosexuals would be committed to a mental institute and subjected to aversion therapy: stripped, administered drugs to make them violently ill, and shown same-sex sexual images as they expelled and lay in their own vomit and feces.

By the beginning of the twentieth century, areas of Germany were socially liberal. Berlin in particular was accepting of homosexuality

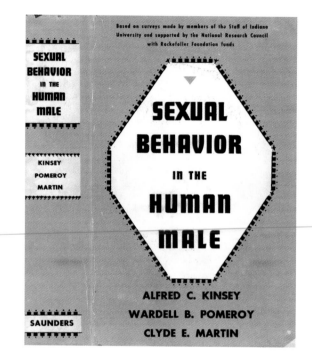

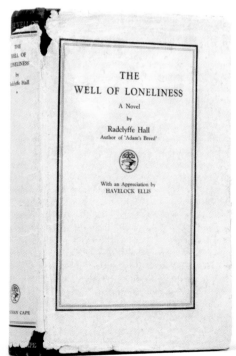

Above: The cover of the groundbreaking 1948 book from Alfred Kinsey et al., which revolutionized how people saw sex and male sexuality.

Left: *The Well of Loneliness* by Radclyffe Hall, published in 1928. An important lesbian classic, it is, however, depressing in the extreme, reflecting the mood of the time.

Opposite: The press reporting of the conviction of Lord Montagu, Michael Pitt-Rivers, and Peter Wildeblood, January 1954. It was a case that outraged some but which also elicited concern at the unfair legal situation of homosexuals.

Previous page: The first annual Christopher Street Liberation Day Parade (now known as Pride), June 28, 1970.

Daily Mirror

THURS
MAR. 25
1954

FORWARD
WITH THE PEOPLE

1½d

No. 15,663

THE MONTAGU CASE

GUILTY

MONTAGU—12 MONTHS'

Pitt-Rivers and Wildeblood each get 18 months'

By PETER WOODS

PITT-RIVERS
Tea in the cells

WILDEBLOOD
Covered his face

THE Montagu case at Winchester Assizes ended in a packed and hushed court yesterday with prison sentences for all three accused.

After a four and a half hour retirement, the all-male jury found Lord Montagu of Beaulieu, 27, his second cousin, Michael Pitt-Rivers, 37, and Peter Wildeblood, 30, guilty of serious offences involving two airmen, Corporal Edward McNally, 25, and Aircraftman John Reynolds, 21.

Mr. Justice Ormerod passed sentences of twelve months' imprisonment on Lord Montagu and eighteen months each on Pitt-Rivers and Wildeblood.

" I am dealing with you in the most lenient way I possibly can," the judge told them.

The jury retired to consider their findings a few minutes after noon. They returned to the packed and tense court four and a half hours later.

The three men in the dock rose to their feet, their faces white with strain.

Outside in the nearby Army barracks a military band struck up a regimental march, its notes stabbing faintly into the words of the Clerk of the Assize as he asked the foreman of the jury for their verdicts on the charges.

" Guilty "........" guilty "........" guilty," said the foreman, and Lord Montagu swayed slightly, pressing his lips together. By his side Wildeblood looked down and covered his face with his hands for a few seconds.

Then, after speeches by the counsel defending the three men, came the sentences.

Standing just below the dock, Lord Montagu's half sister, the Hon. Elizabeth Douglas Scott-Montagu, who had been in court throughout the eight days of the trial, buried her face in her hands.

The set expressions of the three men in the dock did not alter as, with a last look round the court, they turned to the steps to the cells below.

Fifteen minutes later Reynolds and McNally were swiftly driven from the court in a small black police car.

They were booed and jeered by the waiting crowd of 300 people and covered themselves completely with a travelling rug in the back of the car.

Later, in a tiny white-

LORD MONTAGU. . . he talked of a telephone call.

'Give Ann my love...'

walled room, Lord Montagu and his half-sister sat and talked about Ann Gage, the twenty-two-year-old society girl to whom Lord Montagu was engaged until last October.

She is now in New York and Lord Montagu had booked a telephone call to her last night . . .

" Please make the phone call for me," he asked his sister, adding "and give her my love"

" She has been so wonderful and I can't thank her enough."

Then he asked a warder how many pictures he was allowed to have in his cell. "Ten," he was told, and turning to his sister, asked her to send him a picture of his ex-fiancee.

Afterwards the young peer tried to cheer up Wildeblood and Pitt-Rivers over a cup of tea brewed on a small gas stove by one of the warders.

Jokingly he told the warders "No prison could be as bad as going through the Guards Depot at Caterham which Michael (Pitt-Rivers) and I have done."

Shortly after 6 p.m. all three men were taken by car to Winchester Prison, 300 yards away.

Lord Montagu is not at home—See Centre Pages.

MURDER GUNMAN DIES IN FIGHT WITH A P.C.

—see story on Back Page

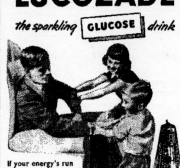

and gender nonconformity, with gay, lesbian, and drag bars attracting a diverse clientele. The first LGBTQ rights organization in the world is believed to have been the Scientific-Humanitarian Committee, founded in 1897 in Germany by Magnus Hirschfeld. The Committee campaigned for international LGBT (specifically including trans) rights, and to overturn Germany's outlawing of gay male sex. Twenty years later, in 1919, Hirschfeld set up the Institute for Sexual Science.

When Hitler came to power, he and his followers raged against the degeneration of public morals. Homosexuality was considered anathema to Nazi plans for a "pure race." On May 6, 1933, Nazi followers ransacked Hirschfeld's academy and around 20,000 books were thrown onto bonfires during the mass book burnings. Hirschfeld was abroad at the time, and stayed in exile. By the following year, the Gestapo had instructed local police to keep a "pink list" of known homosexuals. In 1935, the law, which already outlawed homosexuality, was toughened to make suspected homosexual behavior—or even thoughts—a crime. In the period up until the end of the war, an estimated 50,000 homosexual men were imprisoned, and between 5,000 and 15,000 were sent to concentration camps. It is not known how many perished.

France has had a complex relationship with gay rights. A capital crime for hundreds of years, in 1791, as a consequence of the French Revolution, a new penal code was enacted that didn't criminalize homosexuality. This made France the first country in Europe to effectively decriminalize homosexuality. After 150 years of an equal age of consent, in 1942 the wartime Vichy government lowered the age of consent for straight people to 15 and raised it for homosexuals to 21.

Russia's revolution also provided an opportunity for change. Following the October Revolution of 1917, the Communist Party introduced a new penal code, which, in effect, legalized homosexuality. For the next decade attitudes were mixed, with some hostility but also some moves to support gay people. But from 1927 to 1930 came a hardening of social attitudes. Homosexuality was officially labeled a mental illness, and in 1933, under Stalin's government, male homosexuality was again criminalized.

In 1948, three years after the Second World War (in which gay US Army servicemen were discharged or even imprisoned), American biologist Alfred Kinsey published his groundbreaking report *Sexual Behavior in the Human Male*. It suggested that not only were 10% of American males homosexual, but also that most men were not exclusively heterosexual or homosexual. The publication caused a huge controversy, as did his report of five years later, *Sexual Behavior in the Human Female*. It later emerged that Kinsey was bisexual.

In post-war Britain, Home Secretary David Maxwell Fyfe ordered a crackdown, determined to "rid England of this plague." As stated by

Above right: Alan Turing, the father of modern computing and the man responsible for techniques that enabled the rapid breaking of German codes during the war, was convicted of gross indecency in 1952 and chemically castrated. In 2019, he was voted the greatest person of the twentieth century by BBC viewers.

Right: A plaque commemorating the Compton's Cafeteria riots of 1966, San Francisco. In response to the harassment and arrest of transgender people, the trans and gay clientele picketed the café—three years before Stonewall.

Opposite: Cover of *The Ladder: a Lesbian Review*, the first national lesbian publication, from the Daughters of Bilitis, published from 1956 to 1970.

Overleaf: Between 1933 and 1945, it is believed that the Nazis arrested 100,000 gay men, sentenced 50,000 and sent 5–15,000 to concentration camps.

GENE COMPTON'S
CAFETERIA RIOT 1966

HERE MARKS THE SITE OF GENE
COMPTON'S CAFETERIA WHERE A RIOT
TOOK PLACE ONE AUGUST NIGHT WHEN
TRANSGENDER WOMEN AND GAY MEN
STOOD UP FOR THEIR RIGHTS AND FOUGHT
AGAINST POLICE BRUTALITY, POVERTY,
OPPRESSION AND DISCRIMINATION
IN THE TENDERLOIN.
WE, THE TRANSGENDER, GAY, LESBIAN AND
BISEXUAL COMMUNITY, ARE DEDICATING
THIS PLAQUE TO THESE HEROES OF
OUR CIVIL RIGHTS MOVEMENT.

DEDICATED JUNE 22, 2006

The Ladder
a Lesbian Review

75¢

APRIL 1968

Graham Stewart in his October 2000 article in *The Times*, "The Accidental Legacy of a Homophobic Humanitarian," there were 1,276 prosecutions in 1939. After Fyfe's first year in office, 1951, there were 5,443.

In the US, fueled by post-war paranoia about Communism, new American laws pushed LGBTQ people to the edge of society and sanity, and, as historian David Carter states, forced them to live in "an uneasy state of fear and spiritual suffocation." Senator Joseph McCarthy and others believed that homosexuality constituted a security risk. If homosexual material was mailed to a home address, the postal service would report it to the FBI. Thousands of people were monitored by the FBI and denied jobs or fired from existing ones. Public information campaigns even warned of the danger of homosexuality.

At around the same time, several high-profile cases caused public concern in the UK. In 1952, Bletchley Park computer scientist Alan Turing, pivotal in winning the Second World War, was convicted of gross indecency. In 1953, beloved actor Sir John Gielgud was arrested and convicted of sex in a public toilet. On the night the news broke, actress Sybil Thorndike prepared nervously to go on stage with him, expecting him to be booed off. To everyone's surprise, Gielgud was met with a rapturous standing ovation. The year after, Alan Turing, who had agreed to chemical castration rather than imprisonment, was found dead, believed to have taken his own life. The same year, the youngest peer in the House of Lords, Lord Montagu of Beaulieu, along with Peter Wildeblood and Michael Pitt-Rivers, was convicted, in a storm of publicity, of "conspiracy to incite certain male persons to commit serious offenses with male persons." The Government, realizing the situation was untenable, asked Sir John Wolfenden to investigate what could be done about the dual problems of homosexuality and prostitution. Three years later, in 1957, the Wolfenden report concluded that homosexuality, in limited circumstances, should be decriminalized.

The Homosexual Law Reform Society, made up of Members of Parliament, academics, and other public figures, was established a year later to campaign for implementation of the report, with a supporting group, the Albany Trust, set up to promote homosexual wellbeing.

In the US, the Mattachine Society, which is regarded as the first significant gay rights group (after the brief existence in 1924 of the Society for Human Rights), was founded in 1950 by Communist activist Harry Hay. Although it is seen now by some as conservative in its desire to portray gay people as "just like everybody else," it was Dick Leitsch, Mattachine's New York representative, who would call ten years later for more direct action. In 1952 the *New York Daily News* outed 26-year-old transgender woman Christine Jorgensen, making her an overnight celebrity. In 1955, a lesbian rights and social organization, the Daughters of Bilitis, was formed in San Francisco to support gay and bisexual women, by couple Del Martin and Phyllis Lyon.

The 1960s ushered in a wave of huge social and political change. In the UK in 1962, heterosexual Labour MP Leo Abse pushed forward a bill

Opposite: Born in France in 1910, Jean Genet spent time in prison for petty crime as a teenager. But after becoming friends with and impressing other leading Parisian artists with his writing, Genet went on to be an important figure, writing explicitly and honestly about politics and his life as a pickpocket and sex worker. As a playwright he became a major figure of the theater of the absurd. He is considered an anarchist, rebelling against the dominant socio-political culture.

Below: Customers at San Francisco's Black Cat Bar, 1950s. A popular hangout for Beats, bohemians, and gay men, the Black Cat closed in 1964 after years of police raids, enforcing the law rendering any "resort for sexual perverts" illegal.

To be returned to
HMSO PC12C1
for Controller's Library
Run No. B.S.H.
Bin No. 03.22.06.
Box No.
Year. 1967.

Sexual Offences Act 1967

CHAPTER 60

ARRANGEMENT OF SECTIONS

Section
1. Amendment of law relating to homosexual acts in private.
2. Homosexual acts on merchant ships.
3. Revised punishments for homosexual acts.
4. Procuring others to commit homosexual acts.
5. Living on earnings of male prostitution.
6. Premises resorted to for homosexual practices.
7. Time limit on prosecutions.
8. Restriction on prosecutions.
9. Choice of mode of trial for certain offences.
10. Past offences.
11. Short title, citation, interpretation, saving and extent.

Sexual Offences Act 1967   CH. **60**   1

ELIZABETH II

1967 CHAPTER 60

An Act to amend the law of England and Wales relating to homosexual acts.   [27th July 1967]

BE IT ENACTED by the Queen's most Excellent Majesty, by and with the advice and consent of the Lords Spiritual and Temporal, and Commons, in this present Parliament assembled, and by the authority of the same, as follows:—

1.—(1) Notwithstanding any statutory or common law provision, but subject to the provisions of the next following section, a homosexual act in private shall not be an offence provided that the parties consent thereto and have attained the age of twenty-one years. *(Amendment of law relating to homosexual acts in private.)*

(2) An act which would otherwise be treated for the purposes of this Act as being done in private shall not be so treated if done—

    (*a*) when more than two persons take part or are present; or

    (*b*) in a lavatory to which the public have or are permitted to have access, whether on payment or otherwise.

(3) A man who is suffering from severe subnormality within the meaning of the Mental Health Act 1959 cannot in law give any consent which, by virtue of subsection (1) of this section, would prevent a homosexual act from being an offence, but a person shall not be convicted, on account of the incapacity of such a man to consent, of an offence consisting of such an act if he proves that he did not know and had no reason to suspect that man to be suffering from severe subnormality. *(1959 c. 72.)*

(4) Section 128 of the Mental Health Act 1959 (prohibition on men on the staff of a hospital, or otherwise having responsibility for mental patients, having sexual intercourse with women

---

to implement the Wolfenden report. Protests against the Vietnam War became a template for the power of resistance. The Black Power movement generated acts of civil disobedience such as the 1965 marches from Selma to Montgomery. Mexicans and Puerto Ricans fought against police brutality, and an Eastern spirituality–influenced movement inspired by the transformative power of sex and love spread across America and was embraced by the Beatles. A US presidential commission on the status of women found widespread inequality, while books such as Betty Friedan's *The Feminine Mystique* inspired the second wave of feminism after the Suffrage movement. In the UK, towards the end of the 1960s, women were allowed to sit in the House of Lords and in 1961 the contraceptive pill was made available—first to married women and then, in 1967, to all. That same year, abortion became legal in all of the UK except Northern Ireland.

In 1961, Dirk Bogarde starred in *Victim*, a film about a gay barrister being blackmailed. In 1962 the state of Illinois became the first to legalize consensual sodomy (no other state would legalize it for almost a decade). In 1964, a large feature in *Life* magazine suggested the American public acknowledge "the secret world of the homosexual," which was slowly emerging from the shadows.

Events at three venues in California gave an early indication of the fight back that was just around the corner. In May 1959, there was unrest at Cooper Do-nuts, a small, 24-hour café near Skid Row in Los Angeles, frequented by gay and trans people. In August 1966, the mainly transgender clientele of Compton's Cafeteria in San Francisco rioted after continual police harassment, resulting in the creation of the country's first trans support group, the National Transsexual Counseling Unit. It is said that the two days of riots began after a trans woman threw a cup of coffee over an arresting policeman, with echoes of what would happen three years later in New York. In February 1967, 200 patrons of the Black Cat Tavern in Los Angeles, appalled at police harassment and brutality,

Opposite: The Mattachine Society held the first "homophile" protests. Prominent lesbian activist Barbara Gittings is pictured here on July 4, 1966, picketing Independence Hall, in Philadelphia on the "annual reminder," a precursor to Gay Pride events.

Above: The Sexual Offenses Act 1967 (UK), which decriminalized sex between consenting men, over the age of 21, in private. It was enacted 10 years after the suggestions of the pivotal Wolfenden report.

EARLY GAY BARS

- Clandestine "molly houses" operated in the UK from the eighteenth century

- Zanzibar, Cannes, France (opened 1885)

- The Cave of the Golden Calf, off Regent St, London, UK (opened 1912)

- Berlin in the 1920s had a thriving network of gay bars, clubs and cafés (including the Eldorado, pictured below)

- The Atlantic House, Provincetown, Massachusetts (considered a gay venue by 1920s)

- Double Header, Seattle (opened 1934)

- Café Lafitte in Exile, New Orleans (opened 1933, claims to be the oldest continuously operating gay bar in the US)

- White Horse Inn, Oakland, California (opened 1933, still a gay venue today)

- Black Cat Café, San Francisco, (opened in 1906, began attracting gay people in the early 1940s)

- Julius, Greenwich Village, New York (patronized by gay people by 1950s, openly welcomed them by early 1960s)

particularly on New Year's Eve 1966, staged a peaceful protest.

In 1961, British fashion model April Ashley was outed by tabloid the *Sunday People* as transgender, causing a sensation. Five years later, the first UK trans support group, the Beaumont Society, was established to help individuals and educate the medical establishment.

In 1967, the BBC dedicated two of the programs in its *Man Alive* current affairs series to the experiences of lesbians and gay men. People of different classes were shown struggling to live peaceful lives, let alone fulfill the basic desire for a loving relationship. Playwright and poet Maureen Duffy was one of the first British women in public life to come out as a lesbian, publishing her first openly gay novel in 1966. She appeared on national television, calling for law reform for gay men.

Then, on July 27, 1967, on the recommendations of the Wolfenden Committee—led by a straight man later revealed to have a gay son and commissioned by a Conservative government, from a bill pushed forward by a heterosexual MP and enacted by a Labour government—the Sexual Offenses Act 1967 became law. Sex between two consenting men over the age of 21, in private, in England and Wales, was no longer illegal. This was too late for countless gay men, including playwright Joe Orton, murdered by his sometime partner Kenneth Halliwell two weeks later, no doubt in part because of mental health problems that the times fostered.

But for others a new dawn was breaking. A coalition of different people with different political views had created a ripple that was about to become an unstoppable wave.

Above: Leo Abse, MP for Torfaen, pictured in April 1965. Abse spearheaded a bill that would result in the partial decriminalization of sexual relations between men.

Left: Customers in drag at Berlin's Eldorado nightclub, 1929.

Opposite: Model and socialite April Ashley singing at the Astor Club in London's West End, 1962. One of the first British people to undergo gender reassignment surgery, she was outed by the *Sunday People* in 1961.

MAUREEN DUFFY
AGED 84, THE FIRST BRITISH WOMAN
IN PUBLIC LIFE TO COME OUT AS A LESBIAN

When I first came out to myself in the early 1960s, both gay men and gay women were very much in the closet. There were notable gay male pubs in Earl's Court and Soho, and dotted throughout the capital, but social venues for gay women were much less common knowledge. A series of gay trials of well-known figures, principally of Sir John Gielgud in 1953, had culminated in the setting up of the Wolfenden Committee to look into the whole question of male homosexuality along with seemingly related matters.

So uptight was the closet, due in part to a respectable working class mantra that "you don't talk about such things," that a closely knit group of us of both genders went through the three years of university together without ever knowing that any of the others were gay.

So when I came out to myself, in the belief, held by most British people, that the French were better at sex, or at least more open about it, I turned to Simone de Beauvoir's *The Second Sex* for enlightenment—and I wasn't disappointed. After reading what she had to say, I thought, "Well, that's alright then." But there was still the question of what to do and where to go to find others.

Fortunately my then "partner," to use a contemporary word, knew a gay vicar who invited us to join him and his "boyfriend" at a pub on the Embankment, where we might find someone who knew where the girls went. And that was how I found myself in the Gateways in Chelsea, dancing to the jukebox until closing time. Leaving there could be tricky. Sometimes there would be a group of men waiting outside to shout abuse or even spit at us. Cries of "Come on over here, darlin'," and "I'll show you what it's all about," although seemingly good-natured, could be threatening.

Meanwhile the campaign for the decriminalization of male homosexuality was in full spate. The Wolfenden Committee had reported favorably in 1957. Not only did I strongly believe that the prosecution of male homosexuals was wrong, but also that homosexuality was, and always had been, a facet of human nature. But I was also becoming increasingly aware that although the clamor for the law to change for men was growing louder in all forms of the media, including voices against it giving it an even greater boost, the fact that there were also gay women receded further into the background—as just the left-behinds who couldn't get a man. Finally I decided that I would write a companion book to D.J. West's *Homosexuality*, talking about the jobs we did, and our lives, in an attempt at equality. The very word "homosexuality" was misinterpreted as being derived from the Latin word "homo," meaning "man," rather than the Greek word meaning "same."

Accordingly, I interviewed a selection of gay women with my clunky tape recorder and drew up a synopsis. I gave this to my agent, who arranged a meeting with the publisher Anthony Blond, known to publish some titles thought risqué, such as *The New London Spy: An Intimate Guide to the City's Pleasures*.

However, Blond's view was, "As you don't have a sociology qualification no one will let you do it. Why don't you write a novel instead?" I turned this over on the way home, rang my agent, and told him that was what I was going to do. And so I began *The Microcosm*, banned by the Vatican, put on the Index and banned in Ireland, then banned in South Africa because it showed black and white characters socializing together. But I was also written to by dozens of women thanking me and saying, "I thought I was the only one in the world."

As a result of the publication of that novel I became very much involved in the male campaign—the TV clip of an interview I gave can still be found on the BBC archive.

Wolfenden succeeded in 1967, but even so *Gay News* was prosecuted in 1977 for blasphemous libel with its James Kirkup poem centered on the crucifixion. In reply I published "The Ballad of the Blasphemy Trial" and waited for the skies to fall. But nothing happened. However, the secretary of the National Secular Society was also prosecuted for sending copies of the Kirkup poem through the post. Brigid Brophy and I attended his trial to show our support for him.

Gradually things have opened up in the UK, first with recognized civil partnerships, then same-sex marriage—except in Northern Ireland. But still LGBTQ people in many parts of the world are persecuted, and even tortured and killed.

When I first came out to myself, it was into a completely buttoned-up society where to be gay was stigmatized or at best jeered at. The temptation for many, both women and men, was to hide their terrible or humiliating secret, which set us apart from "normal" society and its norms. The wealthy women of Britain and America, Gertrude Stein, Radclyffe Hall, and many others, holed up in Paris between the wars. For those of us who didn't have that option, we had either to live in secret, or like me, be bloody-minded and brazen it out. So it was I found myself in battle again against Maggie Thatcher's Clause 28 in the 1980s. Then came the AIDS epidemic and I was writing poems to be read at the funerals of three of my friends. We have come a long way, but we must never forget the clock can always be put back.

Above: Maureen Duffy, pictured in the early 1960s.

BISI ALIMI
ACTIVIST AND WRITER, PROFILING
HIDDEN HERO, BAYARD RUSTIN

It was an afternoon in February 2010 and I had just been commissioned to write a piece on iconic Black LGBT people through history. Writing this was a task too big for me. As a young gay man growing up in Nigeria, the idea of an icon was an illusion—like others like me, I was lonely, with no one to look up to. As I delved deep into the article research, I came across someone who would change my life. I saw a video on YouTube titled "The Lost Prophet," telling the life story of a Black gay man who was iconic indeed. He was Bayard Rustin.

The video spoke of his role within the civil rights movement, his following of the teachings of Mahatma Gandhi, and how he influenced the politics of both Martin Luther King Jr. and Malcolm X.

The story of Bayard Rustin, like those of Alice Walker, Marsha P. Johnson, and many other powerful queer people of color is not one you hear often.

Born on March 17, 1912, in West Chester Pennsylvania, he was brought up by Julia and Janifer Rustin, his grandparents. At an early point in his life, he was a member of the Young Communist League before he left to join the Quakers. It was this journey in his life that led him along a path that would enable him to become the face of the August 1963 March on Washington for Jobs and Freedom.

Prior to the march, Rustin faced persecution by the American government, who felt his activism was becoming too challenging for them to curb. Dr. King was put under pressure by the FBI and some members of the civil rights movements to discard him. To the FBI, he was a threat they needed to get rid of, and to the Black civil rights movement, a burden too heavy to carry. The main challenge was that Jim Crow–era America hated gay people and Black people, and Bayard Rustin was a Black man living an openly gay life.

This was a big problem for the heavily religious Black civil rights movement, which was faced with the option of discarding the main strategist behind the movement because of his sexuality, or facing the consequences from many Black people that objected to his sexuality.

Leading up to the March on Washington, Dr. King felt he had no other option but to distance Rustin from the campaign, as congressman Adam Clayton Powell reportedly threatened to accuse Dr. King and Rustin of having an affair. However, without Rustin's dedication to the cause, the movement began to lose steam.

With little option, the movement reinstated Rustin and he organized one of the most successful civil right protests in the history of America. He went on to campaign for gay rights, stating in a 1986 interview with the *Washington Blade* that in the 1940s, "…it was an absolute necessity for me to declare homosexuality, because if I didn't I was a part of the prejudice." Rustin continued his unyieldingly dedicated work as an activist until his death on August 24, 1987, at 75 years of age.

Bayard Rustin's life can be summed up in the words of Rustin himself: "We need in every bay and community a group of angelic troublemakers." Rustin led an angelic troublemaker life, dropping seeds of change wherever he went.

That day in February helped me to see the blackness in my queerness as not just a footnote in history, but as a core of it.

Thank you, Bayard Rustin.

Right: Bayard Rustin, a gay man and friend of Martin Luther King Jr. and a key figure in the American civil rights movement. Pictured in the early 1960s.

CULTURE: LITERATURE

Oscar Wilde died in 1900. He had been released from his imprisonment for sodomy in 1897, and his health never recovered. His works with gay themes, including *The Picture of Dorian Gray*, were successful—despite, or perhaps because of, their notoriety—but it wasn't until the twentieth century that LGBTQ literature began to flourish, and queer themes were brought out of the subtext.

Virginia Woolf wrote what is considered to be one of the key early twentieth-century queer novels: *Orlando*, with a protagonist who moves through time and between genders. The book has been interpreted as a love letter to Vita Sackville-West, and it was a success. It was published in 1928, the same year as Radclyffe Hall's *The Well of Loneliness*, which, in contrast, was banned for obscenity.

French author Jean Genet's debut *Our Lady of the Flowers* (*Notre-Dame-des-Fleurs*), written in prison, is set in the Parisian underworld. It features explicit gay sex and centers around trans character Divine. The novel was first published, anonymously, in 1943. Genet was championed by Sartre and Cocteau, and went on to inspire the Beat Generation writers.

Many LGBTQ writers born after the turn of the century, like Patricia Highsmith and playwright Tennessee Williams, wrote obliquely about their sexuality. Highsmith used a pseudonym for her 1952 radical lesbian novel *The Price of Salt*, which was rejected by Highsmith's usual publisher. The novel was republished as *Carol* under her real name in 1990, just five years before the author's death. She was by no means the only LGBTQ writer to publish under an assumed name, either through choice or necessity.

Some of Highsmith's near contemporaries—Gore Vidal, Christopher Isherwood, and Violette Leduc, for example—wrote more openly about LGBTQ characters. Even so, for a long time openness still meant censure and, in some cases, censorship.

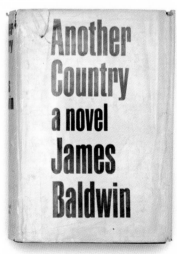

Left: Armistead Maupin, author of the unforgettable *Tales of the City* series, in San Francisco, 1989.

Below: A 1963 hardback edition of James Baldwin's controversial third book.

Opposite: Feminist, author, and activist Audre Lorde giving a lecture at the Atlantic Center for the Arts, Florida, in 1983.

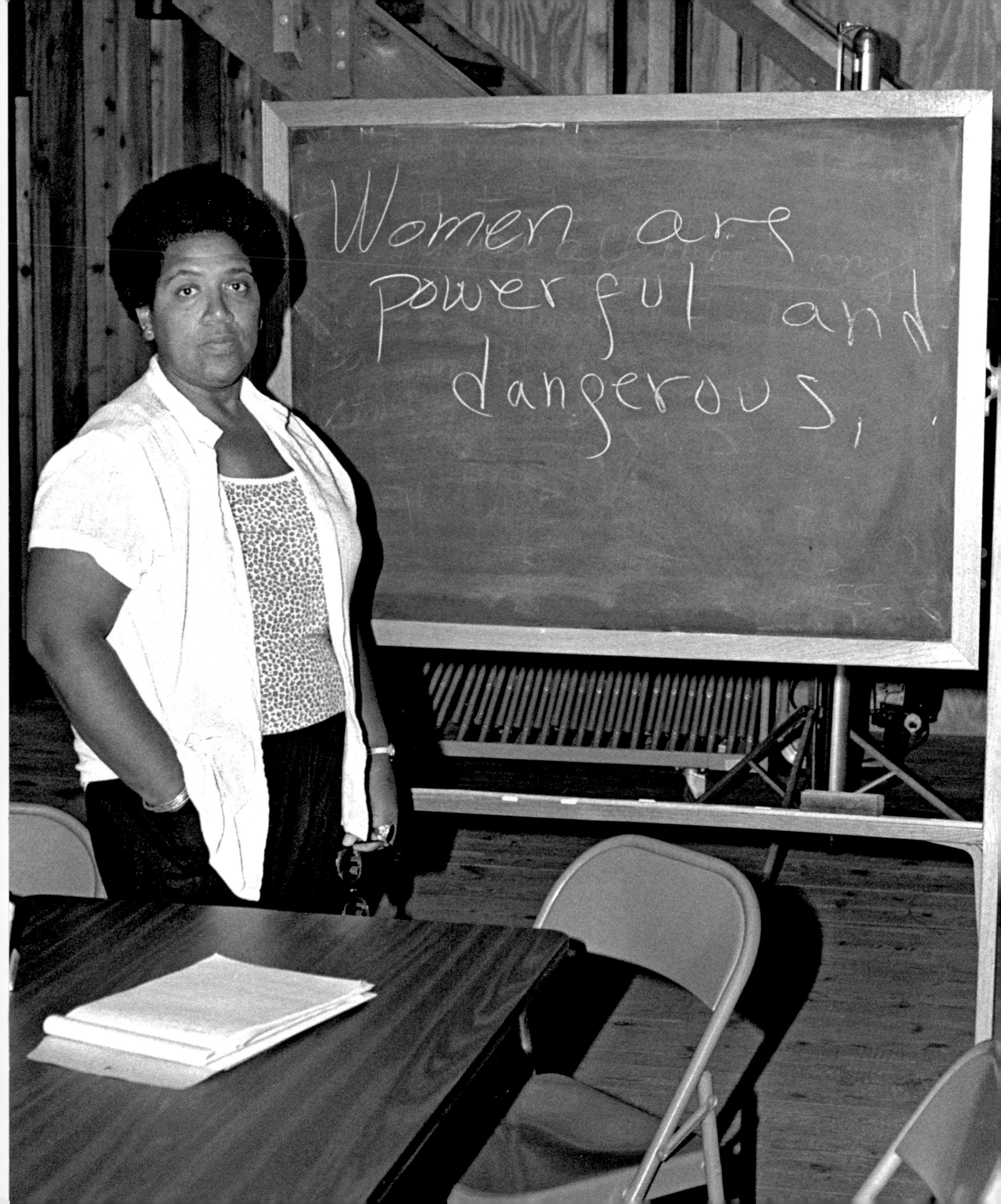
Women are powerful and dangerous,

BONNIE'S STONE WALL

By 1920 certain areas of America were gaining reputations for being more tolerant of homosexuals. According to historian John D'Emilio, significant numbers of gay people had congregated in the French Quarter of New Orleans, San Francisco's Barbary Coast, and in New York, Harlem and Greenwich Village. The Village, in particular, was welcoming of artists— and of others on the outside of mainstream American society. In 1918, the Whitney Studio Club for new artists (which would later become the world-famous Whitney Museum of American Art) opened in Greenwich Village, and America's first racially integrated nightclub, Café Society, opened nearby in 1938.

In 1930 some old stables on Christopher Street between West 4th Street and Waverly Place opened as a tearoom, an edgy, low-rent restaurant and secret speakeasy popular during Prohibition. David Carter, in his essential book *Stonewall* (2004), notes that in the same year, lesbian Ruth Fuller Field, writing as Mary Casal, published an autobiography called *The Stone Wall*. He suggests that a one-time owner might have named her tearoom Bonnie's Stone Wall in an effort to send a subtle signal that women who were like Mary Casal were welcome. As the years passed, it would become known as Bonnie's Stonewall Inn, and by 1960 it had evolved into a fairly respectable, fully fledged restaurant, simply named the Stonewall Inn.

In the mid-sixties, the restaurant was gutted by a major fire and closed. It was at this point that it became, as officially as it could be at that time, a bar for gay people. A local man called Tony "Fat Tony" Lauria, the son of a powerful member of the Genovese family—and a mafioso—decided to reopen it explicitly as a venue for gay people.

At that time, the Mafia ran all of Manhattan's gay bars. The mob did not care for gay people any more than the rest of mainstream society did, but they did care about money. Being illegal, such bars did not have a liquor license and did not pay tax. With just rent and a monthly payment to corrupt police officers to ensure they would allow the venue to operate, gay bars could be a surprisingly good source of income. Fat Tony gave the bar a basic new look—literally painting over the charred interiors with black paint—and on March 18, 1967 the Stonewall Inn opened its doors as a bar for queers, albeit an illegal one.

There were key aspects that made the Stonewall Inn different to other gay bars. Firstly, with two dancefloors, it was bigger than any other gay venue—not only in New York City but also, at that time, in the whole of the US. Secondly, it was on a prominent street, not down an alley

Right: Christopher Street, Greenwich Village, New York City, pictured in 1966. The Stonewall Inn can be seen on the far right. The offices of the *Village Voice* can be seen in the foreground.

as others were. Thirdly, it was cheap. The Stonewall Inn charged an entry fee of just $1 on weeknights and $3 on weekends. As is still the case today, a common part of the gay male experience is of young men migrating from small towns to the freer, bigger, gayer cities. Often having been attacked, ostracized, or thrown out of their homes, many thousands flocked to New York City in the 1960s. These teenagers frequently turned to prostitution or begging, and many were homeless and slept in local parks. The cheap entrance fee meant they could find some solace and safety and, usually, someone to go home with.

But perhaps the most important thing that made the Stonewall Inn unique was the fact that it was the one gay venue in New York where the management would allow people of the same gender to dance together, something which was illegal. In 1967, most of the gay population of New York City would never have seen this before.

Because of all of these factors, the bar immediately gained a large clientele. Most veterans seem to agree that the patrons were predominantly gay and bisexual men. But it's undoubtedly true that they were edgier and more diverse than those of the other gay venues, which tended to be more straitlaced, attracting more discreet, usually white, men, dressing in a more traditionally masculine way. Those kind of men also frequented the Stonewall Inn, but also in the mix were men in drag and make-up, very effeminate men known as "flamers," butch lesbians, people of color, Hispanic people, sex workers, and what we would now call transgender and non-binary folk: the kind of people at the margins of an already marginalized community.

Because of all of this, the Stonewall Inn was a roaring success. As Carter writes, Fat Tony and his cronies made more than the $3,500 they had spent on the refurbishment on the first night alone.

Below: Members of the Mattachine Society—John Timmins, Dick Leitsch, Craig Rodwell, and Randy Wicker—staging a "sip-in" at Julius's Bar, New York City, April 21, 1966. New York liquor laws prevented bars from serving gay customers.

Opposite: Christine Jorgensen found fame in 1952 as the first American known to have gender reassignment surgery. She is shown practicing her ballet number at the Café Society Club, Greenwich Village, New York, c.1960s.

AT THE
INN

At the Stonewall Inn, discretion was vital. Despite the large sign out front, the Mafia owners evaded the illegality of not having a liquor license by pretending the Inn was a kind of private members' club known as a "bottle club." At real bottle clubs, paid-up members would bring their own alcohol that was labeled with members' names, kept at the bar, and served by the staff. In reality, at the Stonewall Inn, you just had to be gay or "look gay," pay the entry fee, and pop your name on a bottle of booze downstairs to give the illusion of it being pre-bought and private. Outside the blacked-out windows onto the street, a doorman known as "Blond Frankie" would vet anyone trying to gain entry. Frankie knew the regulars well and, on the lookout for straight people or undercover police, would ask anyone he didn't immediately recognize to describe the distinctive décor of the bar. If they could answer correctly he'd let them pay their entrance fee and sign in (usually with a fake name), and they'd then be given two tickets, which would be exchanged inside for drinks.

The venue was not safe or hygienic. There were two packed dancefloors but no fire escapes. Drinks were watered down and there was no running water behind the bar. Every night before opening time, two sinks and a rubber tub were filled up with water, in which glasses were rinsed in before being refilled. The fetid water was emptied into overflowing toilets, meaning the floor was often wet. An outbreak of hepatitis was linked to the venue.

Nevertheless, for a crowd who could dance the night away to the music of Martha Reeves and the Vandellas, the Shangri-Las and the Supremes—the music of heartbreak and of hope that love would heal the pain of the outside world—a night at the Stonewall Inn was worth the risks and discomfort.

The popularity of the bar meant there was enough money to pay off the police handsomely. An article in *Pageant* magazine states that the 6th Precinct of the Manhattan Police Department was paid $1,200 from the venue every month. Police officers would arrive at the bar, talk in a friendly manner with the door staff and sometimes have a drink with the owner before disappearing and going back out to their cars. Many, including journalist Craig Rodwell (who dated politician and gay rights activist Harvey Milk when he lived in New York), were outraged that this dysfunctional, corrupt relationship was at the center of the city's gay life.

"Bars have always been our only place, our haven in a sense," he said. "I was always furious that the Mob controls so much of our social life."

But despite lining their pockets, the police still had to be seen to be trying to stop this illegality. Local neighbors would complain regularly about the insalubrious crowd, and at least once a month the police would raid the Stonewall Inn, as they did all gay bars, arresting a handful of patrons or staff.

Some have suggested that the police were getting more serious about closing gay bars. Drugs and sex were sold at the venue, although not by the management. In a time when being gay could get you fired from your job and locked in a mental institution, blackmail was not uncommon. There were allegations that important Wall Street figures had been threatened with outing by men they'd met at the Stonewall Inn. In the weeks before the riots, other bars such as the Snake Pit and the (interestingly named) Sewer had been raided, and a handful, including The Checkerboard and the Tele-Star, had closed down.

According to accounts, the police had such a close relationship with the gay bars that they would often let them know when a raid was going to happen, sometimes carrying them out before the busiest times so the rest of an evening could run smoothly.

In the event of a raid, bosses would make sure they were off the premises and the cash tills were light. When police arrived, the bouncers would press a secret button that would turn the lights on downstairs to warn everyone to stop touching, separate from their dance partners and brace themselves. A handful of people would be arrested, sometimes including the staff, and then the bar would continue, as it had done on the countless nights it had happened before. Those arrested had to worry about having their names published in the newspaper, often outing them to friends, family, and employers. Although raids could be frightening, to some regulars it became mundane, expected—just part of the experience of being a regular at the Stonewall Inn.

But not on the night of Friday, June 27th in 1969.

Opposite: The outside of the Stonewall Inn, pictured in 1969, with its windows boarded up in the immediate aftermath of the riots.

THE NIGHT THEY
BURIED JUDY GARLAND

No one knows for sure why that one raid on that night provoked such a
reaction when so many identical raids before had not.

I n his book *Stonewall* (1993), Martin Duberman notes the global
instability in the two years directly before the riots in an already
volatile decade of energized change. On April 4, 1968, just over a
year before the Stonewall riots, Martin Luther King, a symbol of
emancipation, was assassinated, and people rioted across America. Then
two months later, Senator Bobby Kennedy was also shot dead. Both
were symbols of change through peaceful means. In May 1968, huge
protests erupted across France, which threatened to turn into a full-scale
revolution. Students at the University of Paris had been arguing with
authorities about the half-finished Nanterre campus, which they claimed
was not fit for purpose. Influenced by Marx, Freud, and Sartre, they also
had growing anger against the influence of consumerism, capitalism,
and American culture. Twenty thousand protested on May 6, and were
met with aggressive retaliation from the police: a riot erupted. More
riots occurred in the following days, and eventually nearly two million
workers joined a national strike. President de Gaulle fled the country and
called a general election. These events reverberated around the western
world. Historian Éric Alary summed up the period of May 1968 and the
1960s in general as "a period when audacious moves seemed possible and
during which society profoundly changed."

In August 1968, the police themselves rioted at the Democratic
National Convention, violently attacking anti-Vietnam War protesters.
The month after, feminists stormed the massively high-profile Miss
America Pageant in Atlantic City. On October 2, 1968, 10 days before
the opening of the Olympics (on which the government had spent the
equivalent of $1 billion), at least 44 student protesters in the Tlatelolco
area of Mexico City were shot dead by government snipers.

The feeling in the air around the world among young and
disenfranchised people was that the politics of politeness was dying.
More and more energized gay people felt that the LGBTQ rights
movement was too gentle—almost apologetic—and that the
movement needed to adopt the angry tactics of other groups.

Over the years, people have suggested that the death of Judy Garland
was a factor that provoked the riots. Garland was the greatest gay icon of

Above right: The Moratorium to End the War in Vietnam demonstration,
Washington DC, November 15, 1969.

Right: Feminists protest at the Miss America pageant on September 7, 1968.
Around 200 feminists threw their bras and other feminine products into a
trash can but did not, as has been reported, burn their bras.

Opposite: Students bombarding the police with cobblestones, Paris, May 6,
1968. The Paris student protests against inequality and lack of decent student
accommodation turned into a near revolution.

her generation, the star of a Day-Glo film about a journey from believing you'll find self-esteem outside yourself, only to realize it resides within. A *Time* magazine article from 1967 acknowledged that "a disproportionate part of her nightly claque seems to be homosexual. The boys . . . practically levitate from their seats." There is no doubt she was beloved. Garland died on June 22, 1969 in London aged just 47, less than a week before the Stonewall riots. On the eve of the riots, June 27, her funeral service was held in New York City. The suggestion is that her death pushed the depressed crowd over the edge.

According to David Carter, though, this has little credibility. It was barely mentioned directly afterwards by people who were there, with just one apparently snarky reference in the *Village Voice* newspaper. Carter argues that the young clientele would have seen Garland as old-fashioned and been more interested in the contemporary music of the day, and that the link was created to mock and diminish the political importance of what occurred. Others, agreeing, have said that Garland's death was powerful only in that it symbolized the death of an old-fashioned "passive victim" mentality represented by the worship of a tragic torch singer, giving way to the more empowered, explosive anger of young people. However, self-identified drag queen and activist Sylvia Rivera said years later that there were people in the crowd who had viewed the funeral and had been upset. As cliche as it may sound, many LGBTQ people are disproportionately invested in the strong, defiant female singers of the time. If a hugely popular gay icon such as Madonna or Beyoncé died today, it's fair to say there would be a significant number of people who would be deeply upset. These are the people who vocalize our pain and desire when we cannot. But that's clearly not the main reason the riots occurred.

By summer 1969, the police were becoming more intolerant of the Stonewall Inn. They were unhappy that the Mafia controlled the bar and that drugs were being sold and taken there. Also, significant numbers

of men at that time, including high-profile Wall Street workers, were being blackmailed, threatened with being outed at work and losing their livelihoods. It seems the time was primed for change. America was a powder keg and, as gay people saw that other marginalized groups were no longer willing to accept being silenced, an LGBTQ revolt was in the air and waiting to happen.

That night started as any other night at the Inn would do. The bar had already been raided once that week. Regulars would have been able to relax, as a second raid in one week would be unusual and unexpected.

At around midnight, 47-year-old deputy inspector Seymour Pine from the 6th Precinct of the New York City Police Department held a meeting to brief his officers about the routine raid. They'd done it before, and it would go as normal. Undercover officers would go in to acquire evidence of liquor being sold, of drugs being traded, and of men dressed as women and women dressed as men. They would arrest transvestites, in particular. People would be held. Arrest rates would be raised. Pats on backs would be given.

"They were easy arrests," Pine would say, years later. "They never gave you any trouble."

Pine's squad consisted of two female officers, five male public morals officers, and a male inspector. They left in unmarked police cars, drove to Christopher Street, and parked up. It was an unusually hot night. Greenwich Village was busier than normal.

The plain-clothes officers entered the bar unhindered. Pine waited.

At 1.20 a.m., he gave the signal. The remaining officers walked up to the door of the Stonewall Inn and shouted, "Police! We're taking the place!"

THE STONEWALL RIOTS

Many stories have been told about that night, but David Carter gives the most meticulously researched account in his 2004 book *Stonewall: The Riots That Sparked the Gay Revolution.*

As the police entered, the usual procedures were followed. The lights were turned on, music stopped. Tills were emptied. Couples separated. Disappointment, frustration, and nervousness rippled through the crowd. Those who'd never experienced a raid asked each other what an arrest would mean for their careers and family. People looked for ways out, but officers moved aggressively through the crowd, forcing some patrons into a separate room. Unusually, there was some resistance, but the raid continued.

Non-Mafia staff had their details taken. Lesbians were roughly frisked, and they too complained. Pieces of furniture were smashed. A teenager named Morty Manford is quoted by David Carter as asking himself, "Why do we have to put up with this shit?"

People perceived to be transvestites—to use the period term, with which many people also self-identified—were usually held in the toilets, but this time many physically resisted, saying, "Get your hands off me!" "Don't touch me!" It was this, Deputy Inspector Pine said years later, that made him decide to arrest more people than planned.

After perhaps 20 minutes, those to be released were ordered into single file and IDs and genders were "examined" before people were allowed to leave, one by one, by the front door. But this time, instead of disappearing, they stood and watched. Other local queer people stopped to watch the commotion.

At first, buoyed by adrenaline, the crowd were in good spirits, joking and chanting, camping it up, perhaps even enjoying the drama. As more individuals were allowed out, cheers went up, and some of those leaving performed to the crowd. More police vans arrived, and those arrested started to be loaded into them. A low chant of "we will overcome" broke out. The police handled arrestees roughly, kicking and pushing them. The crowd answered back, calling officers "Lily Law" and other names. Quips and bursts of laughter mixed with a growing tension. The crowd continued to swell. Some banged on the sides of the wagons. Local gay journalist Craig Rodwell yelled, "Gay power!" and was hushed by his friend, but others repeated the cry.

Then, one of the police officers pushed a trans woman—some say it was performer Tammy Novak—who gave him a warning, buoyed on by her friend, possibly Sylvia Rivera. When she was shoved again, Novak hit him with her handbag. In return he hit her around the head with his baton.

Boos rippled through the crowd.

A man in a dark red T-shirt, believed by Carter to be a local Puerto Rican man, shouted, "Nobody's going to fuck around with me! I ain't going to take this shit!"

Opposite: One of the many unsung heroes of the early gay rights movement, journalist and book shop owner Craig Rodwell, with a slogan popularized by Mattachine activist Frank Kameny. Photographed in 1969.

AT FIRST, BUOYED BY ADRENALINE, THE CROWD WERE IN GOOD SPIRITS, JOKING AND CHANTING, CAMPING IT UP, PERHAPS EVEN ENJOYING THE DRAMA.

Various accounts suggest the incident with the handbag was the main flashpoint, along with one other: a butch lesbian of color, since rumored by some to be Stormé DeLarverie, was dragged, after being arrested for wearing male clothing, into the back of a wagon. Fighting with the police, she yelled, "Why don't you guys do something?"

Her queer siblings answered her call, and the crowd erupted. People screamed: "Let's turn it over!" "Pigs!" and "Police brutality!" and threw more coins and the odd bottle. Drag queens kicked police, one stealing his keys to unlock her handcuffs, then passing the keys on. Police fought back, hitting people with their batons. Mayhem broke out. Shocked, Deputy Inspector Pine ordered the three full wagons to leave—and return as quickly as possible—but as they did so, the furious crowd rocked the police vehicles, people hammering on their sides, and at least one had its tires slashed.

We can't be sure who, but someone, likely the Puerto Rican man in the dark red T-shirt rumored to be named Gino, picked up a cobblestone and threw it at a van, frightening the police, who then made the decision to retreat back into the Stonewall Inn, where they struggled to shut the front doors.

With the police caged in, someone threw a garbage can into one of the windows, many of which were already cracking under assault from coins. Glass shattered and the noise of it signaled the riot proper. With the police barricaded into the Stonewall, the anger of the crowd turned into blind rage aimed at reclaiming their bar from the people who had for years been harassing them out of the only safe spaces for LGBTQ people. More cobblestones, coins, bottles, and anything that people could get their hands on were thrown at the windows.

With a sense of mania, the crowd rocked a lamp post out of the ground and used it as a battering ram to smash the door in. Others poured lighter fluid onto rags and threw them through the broken windows. Smoke started to stream from the venue. Inside, Pine and his men extinguished flames as they erupted. Fearing that they'd be burned to death or that the crowd was going to break in and kill them, they drew their guns. Pine, knowing what shots would lead to, shouted at his men to fire under no circumstances, unless he clearly gave the order.

Realizing the gravity of what was unfolding, some of the crowd ran to local public phones, calling friends to get down to Christopher Street as quickly as possible. Activist Craig Rodwell called the local papers to alert them to the unfolding story. Another man, Jim Fouratt, called politically active friends who he thought would support an uprising against the police.

Accounts continue to differ about what role different members of the LGBTQ community played. David Carter quotes a bystander who said it wasn't drag queens but "flame queens," gay men perceived as effeminate and who wore flamboyant shirts and scarves, who led the fight.

It is also true that many "traditionally" masculine gay men took part, too. Though it's often been portrayed as being predominantly led by gay men, many accounts agree that it was the most marginalized—trans people, people of color, men perceived as "effeminate," women perceived as "butch," and street kids—who led the Stonewall riots. Queer street kids in particular, those who had traveled across America to find New York City after being thrown out of their homes by parents and ostracized by their communities, homeless people living around Christopher Street

with literally nothing to lose, threw themselves into the fray, which by then numbered between 500 and 600 people.

Michael Fader, as quoted in David Carter's book *Stonewall*, said, "We all had a collective feeling like we'd had enough of this kind of shit. It wasn't anything tangible anybody said to anyone else, it was just kind of like everything over the years had come to a head on that one particular night . . . Everyone in the crowd felt that we were never going to go back . . . It was time to reclaim something that had always been taken from us . . . We didn't really have the freedom totally, but we weren't going to be walking meekly in the night and letting them shove us around—it's like standing your ground for the first time and in a really strong way, that's what caught the police by surprise."

With the door being bashed in again and again, Pine, fearing for his life, was about to order his men to open fire—something which would have killed rioters and likely guaranteed the death of himself and his officers—when the sirens of reinforcements were heard, and more police vehicles arrived to rescue them.

But this was not the end of the riots. Though Pine's team was saved, the crowd was angry and not dispersing. Garbage cans were set alight and projectiles continued to be thrown. The area around Christopher Street turned into a cat-and-mouse of queer people against the riot-trained police. Objects were thrown; police gave beatings and tried to take as many people away as possible. Other people, including local residents, blocked the roads under the pretense of just watching. The riot police advanced in a tactical V formation, helmets with visors down and batons raised, and found themselves faced with an astonishing sight. A group of street kids had linked arms in a row and started performing a favorite routine, chanting in defiant unison:

> We are the Stonewall girls,
> We wear our hair in curls,
> We wear no underwear,
> We show our pubic hair,
> We wear our dungarees,
> Above our nelly knees!

The street kids stood their ground for longer and longer, letting go and running only at the last minute, with the officers moments from them. The skirmishes continued for the next few hours, eventually dying out when people went home to sleep.

The next day, the electric atmosphere remained. The more political LGBTQ people were rejoicing, with some disappointed that the riot had not moved down towards City Hall, but news spread quickly across New York. Craig Rodwell's calls to the press bore fruit. The *Daily News* placed the riots on its front page, and both the *New York Times* and *New York Post* also carried reports.

During the day on Saturday, June 28, crowds again began to gather in Greenwich Village, some to view the blackened front of the Stonewall Inn, which, as the day progressed, was daubed with slogans such as "Gay power!"

Opposite: One of the only pictures of the Stonewall riots, believed to be from the initial hours of the uprising, in the early morning of June 28, 1969.

The city was abuzz with a new, defiant energy. The Wednesday following the riots, when the *Village Voice* ran what was perceived as a dismissive, homophobic report, a crowd gathered outside threatening to burn their offices down. More fighting and arrests occurred but, as one attendee stated: "The word is out. Christopher Street shall be liberated. The fags have had it with oppression."

In the immediate aftermath, activists knew they could not afford to lose momentum. Raids on gay bars continued, sometimes led by Inspector Pine, and by October 1969, the Stonewall Inn had closed.

There was widespread agreement that radical tactics inspired by the Vietnam protests and the Black Panthers were needed. The Mattachine Society and Daughters of Bilitis were superseded by the Gay Liberation Front: the first activist group to have "gay" in its title. The GLF's aims included wider issues of inequality, including fighting capitalism, and it too was superseded by the Gay Activists Alliance, which focused specifically on lesbian and gay rights.

By that time, Craig Rodwell had been a key figure for around five years—since the Mattachine Society's picket at the White House on April 17, 1965, after which Rodwell had proposed the "Annual Reminder" protest. The first, attended by 39 people, was conservative in tone and dress, but still radical in itself. At a meeting at Rodwell's flat on November 2, 1969 a new proposal was issued in response to Stonewall:

> That the Annual Reminder, in order to be more relevant, reach a greater number of people, and encompass the ideas and ideals of the larger struggle in which we are engaged—that of our fundamental human rights—be moved both in time and location.

> We propose that a demonstration be held annually on the last Saturday in June in New York City to commemorate the 1969 spontaneous demonstrations on Christopher Street and this demonstration be called CHRISTOPHER STREET LIBERATION DAY. No dress or age regulations shall be made for this demonstration.

> We also propose that we contact Homophile organizations throughout the country and suggest that they hold parallel demonstrations on that day. We propose a nationwide show of support.

And so, organized by Craig Rodwell, Fred Sargeant, Brenda Howard ("the mother of gay pride"), Ellen Broidy, Linda Rhodes, and others, Christopher Street Liberation Day, the world's first Gay Pride march, was held in New York City on Sunday, June 28, 1970, to commemorate the first anniversary of the Stonewall riots of 1969.

On that same weekend, marches were held in Chicago, Los Angeles, and San Francisco. Later that year, Marsha P. Johnson and Sylvia Rivera, two self-identified drag queens who had been present at the Stonewall riots, created a new organization called the Street Transvestite Action Revolutionaries, or STAR. Specifically formed to support people on the margins, including gender nonconforming people, sex workers, and homeless people, STAR opened a shelter known as STAR House, originally in a parked truck trailer, later an apartment, which they funded through sex work to offer shelter to those who needed it.

On the last Sunday in June 1971, other cities to hold Christopher Street marches included Boston, Dallas, Milwaukee, Paris, West Berlin, Stockholm, and London. The first official European Pride march was in Münster, Germany, on April 28, 1972.

By 1972, Brighton and London in the UK and Atlanta, Buffalo, Detroit, Washington DC, Miami, and Philadelphia, US, did the same. "Gay Pride" was born—the creation of the term is often credited to Craig Schoonmaker, while bisexual activists Brenda Howard and Robert A. Martin championed its use.

By 1973, the tension between different socio-economic groups, gender nonconforming people, and people of color, and those who wished to present a more middle class (and white), "respectable" face of gayness,

Above: *Marsha P. Johnson* by gay artist and photographer Alvin Baltrop, silver gelatin print, c.1975–86. Johnson was one of the key figures of the Stonewall riots. Gender nonconforming, she has become a symbol of the erasure of trans people and people of color from LGBTQ history.

Overleaf: The Gay Liberation Front marches on Times Square, New York City, 1969.

but it was an arrest in a public bathroom in Los Angeles in 1998 that finally outed him. George would spend the rest of his life talking very openly about his sexuality.

In 1984 came probably the most political of all British gay pop groups of the time. Formed by singer Jimmy Somerville and keyboardists Steve Bronski and Larry Steinbachek, Bronski Beat had the specific intention of being out, loud, and politically gay. "Why?" the first track on their debut album *The Age of Consent*, was a cry of anguish at homophobia. Their classic anthem "Small Town Boy" described an archetypal experience of gay men of the decade. In 1985, Somerville set up new group, The Communards, with Richard Coles, and had hits with "Never Can Say Goodbye," "Don't Leave Me This Way," "There's More to Love (Than Boy Meets Girl)," and perhaps the most moving song ever recorded about AIDS, "For a Friend."

In 1986, flamboyant frontman Andy Bell and musician Vince Clarke as Erasure had the first of an eight-year string of brilliant top hits, which included "Ship of Fools," "Sometimes," and the gay anthem "A Little Respect."

That same year, electronic synth duo Pet Shop Boys began a long succession of artful pop mega hits that dominated the charts between 1986 and 1988 and continued into the late 1990s. The band had high artistic ambitions and sang, in a coded way, about growing up gay in the UK in the 1980s, with songs such as "Rent," "Left to My Own Devices," and "It's a Sin." Having a complicated relationship with homosexuality, as Neil Tennant told me in 2016, they resented the "gay label" but joined protests against Section 28, worked with queer artist Derek Jarman, and in 1994 singer Neil Tennant came out in an interview in *Attitude*, promoting perhaps their most explicitly gay album, *Very*.

The 1990s were still a time when homophobia was rife, but things were starting to change. Madonna, by then the biggest star in the world, brought gay culture directly into the living rooms of the public. She had men dance together in her tours, showed them kissing in her documentary *Truth Or Dare*, French-kissed women in her videos, and included lesbian and gay sex in her book *Sex* (1992), all the time speaking about homophobia in interviews. Canadian singer k.d. lang came out in 1992, and the year after so did US rock singer Melissa Etheridge. Popular American folk singer Janis Ian, who had an American Number One album in 1975, came out as a lesbian in 1993. In 1998, Rob Halford, singer with the 50-million-record-selling metal rock band Judas Priest, acknowledged he was gay in a moving interview with *The Advocate*, in which he said, "Obviously this is just a wonderful day for me." That same year, Israeli trans singer Dana International sensationally won the Eurovision song contest with her song "Diva." The following year, British Boyzone singer Stephen Gately came out, forever smashing the myth that young girls wouldn't buy the records of gay pop stars.

Left above: Frankie Goes to Hollywood wearing their hearts on their sleeves in a risqué shoot for *GQ* magazine, 1982.

Left: Two of the first female music stars to come out: K. D. Lang kisses Melissa Etheridge at a concert benefiting LIFEbeat, a charity that uses music to help tackle issues of sexuality and sexual health, in New York, 1994.

Opposite: Scissor Sisters' Jake Shears in 2018.

JAKE SHEARS
SINGER, SONGWRITER AND
LEAD SINGER OF THE SCISSOR SISTERS

When I was in sixth grade, music seemed to be dominated by Vanilla Ice and MC Hammer and hair metal bands like Mr. Big and Extreme. Then, within months, you suddenly had B52s' *Cosmic Thing* and Deee-Lite's *World Clique*, and I went crazy for them. I didn't know anything about them, but I got the maxi singles on cassette for "Groove Is In The Heart" and "Love Shack" and I wore them out. The moment I saw the opening of the "Groove Is in the Heart" video, with Lady Miss Kier in a fake fur coat, I just froze. I felt like I had seen something that I had been waiting for and I became obsessed with both of those acts. They weren't explicitly queer, but culturally they were very, very queer. Lady Miss Kier has always read to me as being a very queer woman, and with the B's, you had Fred Schneider. Fred's voice is explicitly queer; he's the sound of a gay man. And I loved it. I ran around the school at lunchtime really working on my Fred Schneider impersonation. My parents would leave the house and I would put on the "Power of Love" by Deee-Lite and would just twirl around the house and completely fag out. As a 12-year-old, that was my first exposure to mainstream queer music.

But also Bowie was a really big thing for me. I started listening to him when I was eight. I saw him in *Labyrinth* and I asked my mum if I could get one of his albums, and I got *Let's Dance* on cassette, then *Scary Monsters* and *Lodger*. They were scary and took me to another place. There's lyrics on *Scary Monsters* where he's singing about rounding up all the faggots, but I knew it was a narrative, telling a story about genocide. I found a bio at the library where they had a quote about him sleeping with a guy in high school. And there was "Boys Keep Swinging," a song on *Lodger*—it's such a gay song. There's lyrics about other boys checking you out and this sexy fraternizing, under-the-radar sexuality, that permeates that song. Those records really shaped what I was looking for in music. At the time I didn't know I was gay. I was eight years old, I knew I was into it, and it definitely shaped what I knew, what I would be looking for. They made their own worlds and their own vocabularies and had their own aesthetic. When we were creating Scissor Sisters, that was so important to me. From when we got our first record deal, I envisaged in my head kind of a dark ride, the kind you get at a carnival. I would envision what is the ride that we as a band and our music are going to take people on, and how we would construct a philosophy and a vibe and really be about something. That was really important to me.

Years later, I almost met him. Almost. He came to see one of our shows, but it happened to be one that was low on energy, as happens sometimes, so I was really unhappy he was there that particular night. He left during the encore which is something celebrities sometimes do so they can get out easily before the crowds. He wrote me an email a couple of weeks later, just to say he enjoyed the show. Feeling like a total loser, I kind of didn't believe him, which was all just my insecurity. I wish I had been more relaxed about it, but he is an artist that has meant so much to me since I was a kid. Even to this day, those three albums are probably my three favorite albums of all time. It's still overwhelming that he saw me perform.

FIRST LONDON PRIDE

In the years following the partial decriminalization of gay sex in 1967, London was alive with possibilities. American activists were spurred on by the legislation change, adding to the momentum back in the UK. But despite legal change, life for some became even more oppressive. The government strongly enforced the new legal boundaries. In an article for the *Guardian*, activist Peter Tatchell wrote of "police stake-outs in parks and toilets, sometimes using 'pretty police' as bait to lure gay men to commit sex offenses. Gay saunas were raided. 'Disorderly house' charges were pressed against gay clubs that allowed same-sex couples to dance cheek to cheek." He goes on to state that in 1966, 420 men were convicted of gross indecency. By 1974 the number had risen to 1,711 convictions.

The British march towards lesbian and gay liberation was now unstoppable. In 1970, the Gay Liberation Front formed in the basement of the London School of Economics, and in November of that year, the very first British gay rights rally took place when 150 activists gathered in Highbury Fields in north London. None of the feared arrests took place. In 1971, the GLF staged an action disrupting the Nationwide Festival of Light: a Christian campaign led by Mary Whitehouse and singer Cliff Richard to protest changing values. Protesters kissed, unveiled banners, and set off stink bombs. One branch of the Homosexual Law Reform Society, which had helped facilitate the 1967 law change, evolved into the Campaign for Homosexual Equality and became one of the UK's first significant gay rights organizations, along with the GLF.

On July 1, 1972—the nearest Saturday to the anniversary of the Stonewall riots—the UK's very first official Gay Pride event was held in London. Around 2,000 people marched from Trafalgar Square to Hyde Park, ending with a picnic in the park. The heavily policed rally received bemused looks and some abuse, but there were expressions of support from some onlookers.

The march signaled a tentative new optimism and openness around queer life. The UK's first gay newspaper, *Gay News*, was launched that same year, and in 1974 the first National TV/TS (Transvestite/Transsexual) Conference was held in Leeds. The march and the subsequent reinvigoration also heralded a new era of LGBTQ-friendly venues. Gay establishments in Britain stretched back to the 1500s, through the molly houses of the 1800s, to the 1940s, when certain bars and clubs were known for being frequented by gentleman of a certain flavor. By the 1960s, more and more venues were opening, mostly in London, such as Camden's Black Cap and Islington's King Edward VI. After 1967, the number of gay bars and clubs exploded.

THE MARCH SIGNALED A TENTATIVE NEW OPTIMISM AND OPENNESS AROUND LGBTQ LIFE.

Left: A plaque in Highbury Fields, north London, commemorating the first gay rights demonstration, which occurred in 1970 and saw the impromptu march met with both abuse and applause from the general public.

Opposite: The Gay Liberation Front was formed in New York directly after the Stonewall riots. The first UK meeting was on October 13, 1970, at the London School of Economics. This British flyer, dated February 20, 1971, lists the group's demands.

Overleaf: Homosexuals are revolting! A rare image of one of the first official British Gay Pride marches, June 1974.

20/2/71

THE GAY LIBERATION FRONT DEMANDS:

*that all discrimination against gay people, male and female, by the law, by employers, and by society at large, should end,

*that all people who feel attracted to a member of their own sex should know that such feelings are good and natural,

*that sex-education in schools stop being exclusively hetero-sexual,

*that psychiatrists stop treating homosexuality as though it were a problem or a sickness, and thereby giving gay people senseless guilt-complexes,

*that gay people be as legally free to contact other gay people, through newspaper ads, on the streets, and by any other means they want, as are heterosexuals, and that police harassment should cease right now,

*that employers should no longer be allowed to discriminate against anyone on account of their sexual preferences,

*that the age of consent for gay men be reduced to the same age as for heterosexuals,

*that gay people be free to hold hands and kiss in public, as are heterosexuals.

ALL POWER TO OPPRESSED PEOPLE !

KEY PROGRESS IN THE 1970S

1970

First Christopher Street Liberation Day march, New York City

1971

Society Five, LGBTQ rights group, formed in Melbourne, Australia

1972

Norway decriminalizes same-sex sexual activity

Sweden allows people to legally change gender.

Hawaii repeals its sodomy laws.

South Australia allows a "consenting adults in private" defense.

East Lansing and Ann Arbor (Michigan) and San Francisco (California) allow gay rights ordinances to pass.

The Quakers' Committee of Friends issues the supportive "Ithaca Statement" on bisexuality.

1973

Malta decriminalizes homosexuality.

Pride Week 1973, Canada's first major LGBTQ pride celebration, took place in several Canadian cities.

Australia and the USA declassify homosexuality as an illness.

1974

The Brunswick Four are arrested in Canada, rousing the LGBTQ community into action.

1975

California and Washington state decriminalize homosexuality.

The American Christian Cause is formed to politicize the Christian right and oppose the "gay agenda."

California and South Australia legalize homosexuality.

Melbourne hosts Australia's first National Homosexual Conference.

1976

Australia forms Homosexual Law Reform Coalition.

Australian Capital Territory decriminalizes homosexuality between consenting adults.

1977

Croatia, Montenegro, Slovenia, and Vojvodina decriminalize same-sex sexual activity.

Harvey Milk is elected to the San Francisco Board of Supervisors.

1978

American artist Gilbert Baker designs the rainbow flag as a symbol of LGBTQ pride.

Transnational International Lesbian and Gay Association founded.

1979

The first National March on Washington for Lesbian and Gay Rights takes place.

Members of the Swedish Federation for Lesbian, Gay, Bisexual, and Transgender Rights (RFSL) protest the classification of homosexuality as an illness; some even called in "sick with homosexuality," resulting in the National Board of Health and Welfare removing the classification.

Above: The rainbow flag is a symbol of gay and LGBT pride and of the LGBTQ movement. A friend of Harvey Milk, Gilbert Baker, was inspired to create it for use as a symbol of peace and also as "the flag of the human race," partly inspired by gay activist Allen Ginsberg. It was first flown at the San Francisco Gay Freedom Day Parade in 1978. The colors represent the diversity of our community and also have specific meanings, according to Baker. Pink = sex; red = life; orange = healing; yellow = sunlight; green = nature; turquoise = magic/art; deep blue = serenity; purple = spirit. Pictured here is one of the first limited edition run of Baker's original rainbow flags, signed in the bottom right corner.

YOU GOTTA GIVE 'EM HOPE

HARVEY MILK: THE MAYOR OF CASTRO STREET

One of the thousands of gay immigrants to San Francisco in the 1960s was Harvey Milk, a man born in 1930 in a suburb of New York to Lithuanian Jewish parents, whose life and legacy would come to be forever entwined with the city of San Francisco and the gay freedom it represents.

It wasn't until 1969, the same year as the riots, that Milk first saw the city, accompanying his then-boyfriend, a stage manager with a production of *Hair*. He returned three years later with a new boyfriend, and they opened a camera shop in Castro Street, the main gay area of the city.

Milk's frustration with President Nixon (he had been a Republican in his younger days), local politics affecting small-business owners, and a gay community that he saw as too conservative pushed him into running for a position on the city's Board of Supervisors. He later remarked, "I finally reached the point where I knew I had to become involved or shut up."

In his first attempt in 1973, Milk came tenth out of 32 candidates. But this forged a relationship with the gay community, who began referring to him as "the mayor of Castro Street." In 1975, he ran and lost again, this time coming seventh and catching the attention of new mayor, George Moscone, who gave him his first, brief political job, on the Board of Permit Appeals. Finally, on his third attempt, on November 8, 1977, Milk was elected onto the Board of Supervisors,

becoming the first openly gay elected official in California history and the first non-incumbent out gay man to be elected to public office in the United States.

Milk made a huge impact in the short time he held office. With his friendly, flamboyant manner, he represented a new way of doing things. He campaigned explicitly and vocally for gay rights and those of other minority groups, as well as for protecting San Franciscan neighborhoods against corporate expansion. He urged people over and over to come out and made vital alliances with the wider community. One of his highest profile campaigns was against anti-gay activist and former singer Anita Bryant and the Briggs Initiative, which would

have outlawed gay people from being teachers. The Briggs Initiative was voted down, and although Bryant had some success, the media attention allowed Milk to bring his message of gay rights to a mass, television-watching audience.

Milk also made enemies. When he went back on an agreement to help fellow supervisor Dan White, a 32-year-old former policeman, to block the opening of a mental health facility in his local district, White refused to speak to him again and was the only supervisor to vote against Milk's 1978 gay rights ordinance. Later that year, struggling on his meager salary and with a failing restaurant business, White resigned his position as supervisor, only to subsequently change his

mind and ask that the Mayor give it back to him. Milk was among those who lobbied Moscone not to do so. On November 27, 1978, White climbed through a window into City Hall and shot and killed the Mayor. He then walked to Milk's office, asked him to step inside, and fired four bullets into him: one in his wrist as Milk raised his hand to protect himself, two in his chest, and two in his head. Both Moscone and Milk died instantly.

Opposite and above: Milk pictured at his camera shop on Castro Street, San Francisco, 1977.
Opposite right: Letter to President Jimmy Carter from Milk, June 28, 1978, calling for his opposition to California Proposition 6, also known as the Briggs Initiative.

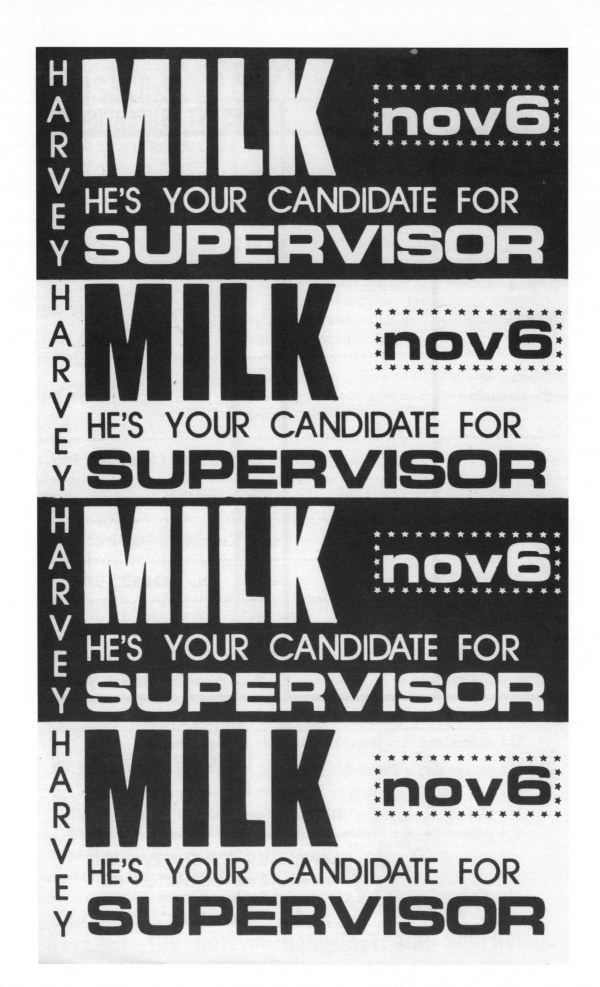

"I KNOW THAT YOU CANNOT LIVE ON HOPE ALONE, BUT WITHOUT IT, LIFE IS NOT WORTH LIVING. AND YOU . . . GOTTA GIVE 'EM HOPE."

HARVEY MILK

When Dan White was convicted on May 21, 1979 of voluntary manslaughter rather than first-degree murder, on the grounds of diminished mental capacity due to depression—supposedly demonstrated by his diet of junk food, in the much-derided "Twinkie Defense"—the city erupted into what has been called the "White Night riots." Two years after his release from his five years served, Dan White took his own life.

Harvey Milk died at just 48, but his legacy is immense. A plaza in San Francisco, where the rainbow flag flutters, bears his name, as does a New York school for LGBTQ youth. Various works of art have been made about him, including an opera, the 1984 documentary film *The Times of Harvey Milk*, and the 2008 film *Milk*, directed by Gus Van Sant, starring Sean Penn and written by Dustin Lance Black, who won the Academy Award for Best Original Screenplay. In 2009, in one of his first acts of office, President Obama awarded Harvey Milk the nation's highest civilian honor, the Presidential Medal of Freedom. Stuart Milk, Harvey Milk's nephew and founder of the Harvey Milk Foundation, accepted the medal.

Harvey Milk's biggest legacy is that of hope. He knew the key was in people coming out. Knowing he might be a target, he recorded a taped message, which stated, "If a bullet should enter my brain, let that bullet destroy every closet door." In 1978 at the city's Gay Pride parade, months before he was assassinated, he made a speech that resonates as powerfully today as it did 40 years ago:

"And the young gay people in the Altoona, Pennsylvanias, and the Richmond, Minnesotas, who are coming out and hear Anita Bryant on television and her story. The only thing they have to look forward to is hope. And you have to give them hope. Hope for a better world, hope for a better tomorrow . . . And if you help elect . . . more gay people, that gives a green light to all who feel disenfranchised, a green light to move forward. It means hope to a nation that has given up, because if a gay person makes it, the doors are open to everyone."

Opposite: Artwork created for Harvey Milk's campaign. He eventually won the office of Supervisor on November 8, 1977, and served for 11 months until his murder on November 27, 1978.

Right: The front page of the *San Francisco Chronicle* on November 28, 1978, announcing the murder of both Harvey Milk and Mayor George Moscone. Murderer Dan White is pictured after his arrest.

THE EARLY 1970S
AND THE NAKED CIVIL SERVANT

The 1970s saw growing change across the world. In 1973, the Australian and New Zealand College of Psychiatry Federal Council and then the American Psychiatric Association both removed homosexuality from their list of mental disorders. (In the case of the US, this was largely due to the research and advocacy of Evelyn Hooker.) In 1974, lesbian Kathy Kozachenko became the first openly gay person in America to be elected to public office when she won a seat on the Ann Arbor, Michigan, city council. That same year, America's first support group for bisexual people, The Bisexual Forum, was set up by Dr. Fritz Klein in New York. In 1973, state sodomy laws were repealed by Ohio, one of 20 American states to do so in the 1970s.

In 1975, one of the most significant queer people of the era came to public attention. Denis Pratt was born in 1908 in Sutton, south London, and went to school in nearby Epsom, Surrey. He dropped out of his journalism course at King's College London and, in his early twenties, moved to central London to study art, began wearing outlandish clothes and make-up, and worked as a sex worker. It was then that he changed his named to Quentin Crisp.

Quentin, with his effete manner, dyed hair, and made-up face, became a recognizable figure in parts of London, mixing with street people and male escorts, sometimes making friends and having sex with the tough men he was so attracted to, but often being beaten up. Not allowed into the army on account of his "sexual perversion," he spent the Second World War in London, made up with hennaed hair, finding affection where he could, especially with his favorites, American soldiers. His love of writing persisted and, after securing an agent, his books began to publish. His third, a memoir initially titled *I Reign in Hell* (after the quote from Milton's *Paradise Lost*: "Better to reign in hell than serve in Heaven"), was published in 1968 as *The Naked Civil Servant*. The book caught the attention of original *Doctor Who* producer Verity Walker, who commissioned a TV adaptation. It was broadcast in 1975 in the UK and US, making an overnight star of Crisp—and of the actor who played him, John Hurt.

The huge notoriety this brought Crisp led to further books, one-man shows, and film appearances that would afford him significant celebrity for the rest of his life, which was mostly spent in New York, living in squalor, accepting social invitations from anyone who would buy him dinner. Quintessentially British, he famously didn't clean his apartment, saying, "After the first four years the dirt doesn't get any worse." Sting's song "An Englishman in New York" is about him. But there was also much controversy: in an interview he referred to AIDS as "a fad" and activist Peter Tatchell alleges Crisp told him he did not believe in rights for homosexuals. "What do you want liberation from? What is there to be proud of?" he apparently asked.

That said, many LGBTQ people of the era, including Boy George, have said that in a world starved of gay representation, Quentin Crisp

was hugely significant to them. Some were burdened with being called "Quentin" by school bullies, but Quentin Crisp was one of the first and most famous out gay people of the twentieth century and certainly, controversy included, one of the boldest and most curious. He died on November 21, 1999 in Manchester, England, about to start a tour of the home country that he despised. His ashes were flown back to New York.

Above: Quentin Crisp photographed with actor John Hurt in costume as Crisp, during the filming of *The Naked Civil Servant*, which aired on UK and US television in 1975.

Opposite: Quentin Crisp aged 40 in 1948. He said of his home years later, that he didn't ever dust it. He said "There is no need to do any housework at all. After the first four years the dirt doesn't get any worse."

CULTURE:
NIGHTLIFE

Towards the end of the 1970s, two gay African American men changed the
course of gay clubbing and dance music across the world.

In 1977, DJ Larry Levan was resident at an invitation-only club called Paradise Garage, held in a warehouse above a parking garage in Hudson Square, New York, while in Chicago DJ Frankie Knuckles was resident at a new venue: a former factory on Jefferson Street in Chicago called Warehouse. Both became the most popular clubs in their respective cities, and the music genres "garage" and "house" evolved directly from the styles of these two original superstar DJs. Both catered for predominantly black and Latino gay men and set the template for what nightclubs would be like for the next 30 years.

In the UK, the late 1960s saw the proliferation of gay bars, including Apollo, The London Apprentice, The Princess of Prussia, the Kings Head, the Pink Elephant and The Regency Club. Le Deuce was an unofficial gay nightclub where mods would dance together. The London gay nightclub

Bang!—later renamed G-A-Y—opened in 1976 at the Sundowner, underneath the Astoria Theatre on Charing Cross Road, providing a sense of community, thanks to its 1,000-strong capacity.

Le Palace, in Paris's 9th arrondissment, was a theater turned club, a magnet for the cool and beautiful, regardless of sexuality, class or skin color. Launching in March 1978 with a performance by Grace Jones, the fashion crowd mingled with celebrities and hedonistic gay party-goers,

Above: Heaven nightclub in Charing Cross, London, has been a popular LGBTQ venue since opening in 1979. Its always-full dancefloor is pictured here in October 1992.

Opposite: Dancing at the Palace in Paris, France, which was opened by Fabrice Emaer in 1978 and known as a bastion of underground culture and avant-garde fashion.

clinking champagne and air kissing, and for the first time, along with Heaven and Studio 54, made being gay seem like something that everybody wanted to be a part of.

At the end of the 1970s, a game-changing club opened in London, whose iconic name would become famous across the world as a symbol of freedom, debauchery, and relentless, fabulous disco. Gay British entrepreneur Jeremy Norman, who had spent time in the US, wanted to create a glamorous and decadent nightclub for London. Norman opened the fashionable Embassy—the UK's answer to Studio 54—in 1978, and in December 1979, underneath the arches next to Charing Cross station, he opened Europe's biggest gay club: Heaven.

Heaven was an overnight sensation. The venue rostered cutting-edge DJs such as Tony De Vit and Warehouse's Frankie Knuckles, led by the Hi-NRG producer Ian Levine. In just a decade, gay clubs in both America and London had gone from being illegal to the coolest places to be. As DJ Luke Howard commented in an article for *Faith Fanzine*, the *Evening Standard* said in a review of Heaven's opening

night that "Heaven's biggest headache could be in deterring London's non-gay discophiles, who could end up trying to pass for gay to get past the elegant bouncers at the disco's equivalent of the Pearly Gates." Purchased, perhaps surprisingly, by Richard Branson in 1982, Heaven would become a cultural touchstone during the 1980s, renowned for the intensity of its partying.

Gay venues have always been about a level of partying only those who have been repressed can comprehend, and sex clubs such as Mineshaft and The Anvil in NYC were wildly popular. Drugs were also a mainstay of many major gay clubs. First cocaine, then ecstasy, then speed and ketamine came to define the experience of clubs such

Above: DJ Larry Levan in 1979, during his decade-long residency at New York's Paradise Garage, where stars such as Madonna and Grace Jones performed in the 1980s.

Opposite: Notorious Berlin superclub Berghain, 2007.

Overleaf: Flyer for Berghain's smaller and more relaxed upstairs space, Panorama Bar.

HISTORIC LGBTQ NIGHTS AROUND THE WORLD

The Abbey, West Hollywood, US. Since opening in 1991, the coffeehouse, restaurant and bar has provided a focal point for LA's LGBTQ community.

Arena Madre, Barcelona, Spain. The flagship branch of the Spanish gay club empire has been hosting themed parties for over 20 years.

Berghain, Berlin, Germany. Now one of the most hardcore and infamous venues in the world. Not for the faint-hearted.

The Cubbyhole, New York City, US. The infamous and much-loved lesbian venue opened in 1994.

Duckie, London, UK. Innovative performance club Duckie, launched by Amy Lamé and Simon Strange in 1995, is still held every week at the historic Royal Vauxhall Tavern.

G-A-Y, London, UK. G-A-Y at the Astoria became so popular that the brand went on to open two venues in London and one in Manchester.

The Imperial Hotel, Sydney, Australia. A rare and refreshing venue where all members of the LGBTQ community mix.

Paradise Factory, Manchester, UK. The northeast of England's most iconic gay club, opened in 1993, was a place where gay and straight could party together.

Popstarz, London, UK. DJ Simon Hobart changed the tempo of gay London with this night, focused on boozing and snogging rather than dancing and drugging.

Le Queen, Paris, France. Global superstar DJ David Guetta got one of his first big breaks here, working as musical director of the legendary club from 1992 to 1995.

Spijker Bar, Amsterdam, Netherlands. The city's oldest gay venue, originally for the leather crowd, now hosts bingo and drag events.

Studio 54, New York City, US. Not strictly a gay club, but the queer vibe was crucial to the iconic venue's appeal.

Woody's and Sailor, Toronto, Canada. One of the most dependable, enduringly LGBTQ venues in the world.

as New York's Sound Factory, which opened in 1989 with DJ Junior Vasquez, and from the mid-1990s Twilo. Laurence Malice's original London all-nighter Trade exploded into the scene in 1990, setting a new trend of the drug-fueled party that it seemed would never end— but it did, when the club closed in 2008.

Historically, bars and clubs were the only places LGBTQ people could meet friends or a prospective partner and feel safe, but with the coming of the Internet and then dating and hook-up apps such as Grindr, the community started to shun bars in favor of technology. Coupled with skyrocketing rents, gentrification, and, sometimes, an atmosphere of unfriendly body fascism that no longer appealed to LGBTQ communities, many gay bars and clubs shut their doors in the early 2010s, a trend that has hit the already small number of lesbian bars much harder, with the last lesbian bar in San Francisco closing in 2015. But as much-loved venues close, some new ones have still managed to spring up, and in some cases, continued to be the tastemakers of club culture. In order to survive, they have had to innovate.

Superclubs such as Berghain, notoriously sexually louche and the epicenter of the techno scene, are at the forefront of a renaissance of gay culture in Berlin. In London, smaller independent venues such as The Glory and Dalston Superstore, along with fun and performative nights such as Sink the Pink, have revitalized the scene. In Paris, club nights and parties at eclectic venues—such as Cocorico, Trou Aux Biches, Menergy and more—have become fashionable. The opening of these new venues and a shift of focus away from shirtless machismo and drugs problems that have destroyed much gay nightlife around the world, there is once again an emphasis on LGBTQ venues as safe harbors, especially for those expressing newfound queer identities.

Opposite: During a time of fear, homophobia and intense hysteria, people with HIV and AIDS were shunned and termed "terrorists." In April 1987, Princess Diana was the first global figure to publicly shake hands with a person with AIDS as she opened the Middlesex Hospital's HIV and AIDS wing.

Above: A billboard advert in London as part of the British government's 1986 HIV and AIDS public health campaign.

Above: ACT UP demonstration, in a protest style known as a "die-in," on World AIDS Day in 1994, in front of the Arc de Triomphe in Paris, France.

Right: ACT UP march in Paris, 1993. Their banner features the name of a number of French AIDS charities and activist groups, and declares "Stop AIDS!"

by 20% to around $6,400 a year. In December 1989, ACT UP staged the "Stop the Church" protest against Catholicism's homophobia and resistance to condoms and women's fertility rights, which saw more than 4,500 people protest outside St Patrick's Cathedral. More than 100 people were arrested.

ACT UP was a flare that shot high over the States, but the group had chapters across the globe. Their presence in London was strong, and included journalist Paul Burston, whose activities as part of the group, including taking part in road blocks, are described in Alexis Gregory's 2018 play *Riot Act*. ACT UP also had a significant presence in Paris. Formed in 1989, the organization staged actions such as "die-ins," hanging an enormous banner over Notre-Dame Cathedral in protest of the Catholic Church's stance on HIV, and handing out sex education leaflets to schoolchildren. In 1992 they staged a "day of despair," conducting various coordinated actions across the city, and the year afterwards, on World AIDS Day, famously covered the obelisk of the Place de la Concorde with a giant condom. The award-winning 2017 film *120 Beats Per Minute*, directed by former member of the organization Robin Campillo, is an urgent and visceral fictionalized account of the Parisian movement.

In 1987 President Reagan first spoke publicly about AIDS and formed the Watkins Commission—the President's Commission on the HIV Epidemic—partly because the actions of ACT UP and other activist groups made it impossible for him to ignore the crisis any longer.

In 1988, 20 years after his death, researchers re-examined the stored tissue of teenager Robert Rayford and identified him as the first known person to die of AIDS in the US. Norwegian Arne Røed and his wife and daughter were identified as the first deaths in Europe, indicating that HIV was present in both Europe and the US at least as early as the 1960s. Scientists later concluded that the virus had passed from African primates to humans in the early twentieth century.

The deaths of celebrities from HIV/AIDS brought attention to the scale of devastation and also lessened the stigma felt by those outside the public eye who had been diagnosed. In 1989 acclaimed choreographer Alvin Ailey died aged 58. In 1990, Ryan White, aged 18; LGBTQ activist Vito Russo, aged 44; artist Keith Haring, aged 31; and Brazilian popstar Cazuza, aged 32, all died from AIDS-related illnesses. In 1991, Queen singer Freddie Mercury died aged 44, just 24 hours after confirming press rumors he had the disease. In the same year, *Beauty and the Beast* and *Little Mermaid* lyricist Howard Ashman died aged 41, and basketball player Magic Johnson told the world he was HIV-positive.

In 1992 AIDS-related illnesses caused the deaths of bisexual *Psycho* actor Anthony Perkins, aged 60; *Brady Bunch* actor Robert Reed, aged 59; beloved British actor Denholm Elliott, aged 70; and Australian singer Peter Allen, aged 48. In 1993 heterosexual tennis champion Arthur Ashe, aged 50, and Rudolf Nureyev, aged 54, both died from the illness.

By 1994 AIDS had become the leading cause of death in Americans aged 25–44. That year author Randy Shilts, aged 42; filmmaker Derek Jarman, aged 52; NWA rapper Eazy-E, aged 30 (who died just a month after testing HIV positive); activist Elizabeth Glaser, aged 47; and British Olympic Champion skater John Curry, aged 44, all died of the illness, and Olympic diver Greg Louganis came out as HIV-positive.

On 30 June 1994, the first episode was aired of the third season of popular MTV reality show *The Real World*, this time set in San Francisco.

ITALY IN THE 1980S

Activists in Italy during the 1980s struggled to make progress in one of the most strictly Catholic and conservative countries in western Europe, with a historically complicated relationship with homosexuality (gay sex has been legal since 1890 and the age of consent is 14 for both gay and straight people). Italy's first gay rights group, Arcigay, was established in Palermo in 1980 and then nationally in 1985. The group is Italy's largest LGBTQ organization today, conducting research and campaigning for full equality for LGBTQ people, and was instrumental in helping Italy legalize same-sex marriage in 2016. As you might imagine, the group spends a significant amount of time protesting the Roman Catholic Church and the Pope, and has an "LGBTI Political Watch" to keep track of public officials' and political parties' stance on relevant issues. Research has shown that social attitudes toward LGBTQ people in Italy are improving, with studies in the last decade suggesting around 74% of the public believes that gay people should be treated the same as others and nearly 80% believes trans people should have legal protection from discrimination.

One housemate succeeded in piercing through prejudice and stereotypes, and got through to viewers all over the world. The housemate, a 22-year-old gay man named Pedro Zamora, was born in Cuba. Zamora had moved to America at the age of 8, tested HIV-positive at the age of 17, and committed his life to educating people about the disease. He decided to audition for *The Real World* in order to inspire compassion for people living with HIV and AIDS, and to increase the public's understanding of living with the disease. As an immensely popular character on the show, he did just that. During the series, Zamora exchanged vows with his partner Sean Sasser, winning over his fellow housemates—and MTV viewers. Audiences of all kinds were gripped by his story. Years later, *Time* magazine ranked Zamora's conflict with his housemates Number Seven on their list of "32 Epic Moments in Reality-TV History." The show aired months after filming, as Zamora was becoming increasingly ill. He died of AIDS-related illnesses hours after the last episode was broadcast, on November 11, 1994. Despite his brief life, Zamora changed public opinion, and the relationship of young Americans with a group of people they had been told were second-class citizens, and whose lives and deaths didn't matter. President Bill Clinton was among those to praise Zamora for his activism, crediting him with giving HIV and AIDS a relatable face and humanizing those living with AIDS.

Previous pages: Two costumed attendees of the 1987 Paris Pride parade, wearing the pink triangle horrifically utilized by the Nazis to identify gay prisoners, and since reclaimed by the LGBTQ rights movement, most prolifically by ACT UP.

Opposite: Cuban-American Pedro Zamora featured on this Spanish-language AIDS prevention poster in the 1980s. Pedro's quote says: "When I turned 17, I found out that I had HIV and also that everyone could get it."

"**Al** cumplir los 17, me enteré que tenía el HIV y también que todo el mundo lo puede contraer."

Peter Zamora, con resultados positivos del HIV

De cada 250 estadounidenses, uno está infectado con el HIV.

1-800-344-7432 **AMERICA RESPONDE AL SIDA**

DEPARTMENTO DE SALUD Y SERVICIOS HUMANOS **CDC**
Servicio de Salud Pública

Less widely known, but also a key documentarian of twentieth century queer life, is Alvin Baltrop. Born and raised in New York, Baltrop began his photography career as a teenager, shooting his native city. After serving as a medic in the Navy, during which time he built his own darkroom and photographed fellow sailors, Baltrop returned to New York and created thousands of images of visitors to the Lower West Side piers between 1976 and 1985. He immortalized a diverse LGBTQ community and a now-lost location that was once a hub for artists and writers. As a Black queer man, he experienced both homophobia and racism from the art world, and his work was recognized for its social and artistic significance only after his death in 2004. Baltrop's photographs are collected in a book, *The Piers* (2015), which is considered a rare document of the pre-AIDS, clandestine sexual culture of New York.

Other key figures of the latter part of the twentieth century art scene in the US include Keith Haring, Catherine Opie, Robert Mapplethorpe, and Nan Goldin. Graffiti artist Haring produced public work, most famously in New York's subway, and found fame and celebrity friends, including Andy Warhol and Madonna. He was an active participant in ACT UP until he died from AIDS-related illnesses in 1990 at the tragically young age of 31, but his work's popularity has never waned, becoming synonymous with humanity, love, and the importance of activism.

Catherine Opie's work has focused on community since she began taking photographs of her family and neighborhood as a child. In the 1990s, her photographic series *Being and Having* (1991) and *Portraits* (1993–1997) depicted LGBTQ people in San Francisco and Los Angeles, focusing on an exploration of the nature of gender identity and queer subcultures by using and subverting traditional portrait formats to challenge the male gaze.

Born in 1946 in New York City, Robert Mapplethorpe took explicitly sexual photographs of himself and other men in the BDSM scene in the early 1970s, causing a sensation. His later intimate portraits are some of the most recognizable of the beautiful people of New York at the time, including Truman Capote, Marianne Faithfull, Grace Jones, Iggy Pop, and the photographer's long-time muse Patti Smith. A touring exhibition of his work, *The Perfect Moment*, caused national controversy and debate from its opening in December 1988, resulting in the publicly funded exhibition being pulled in 1989. By that time, Mapplethorpe had died from AIDS-related illnesses, on March 9, 1989.

Nan Goldin's photographs are arguably the most influential, and certainly the best-known, visual documents of LGBTQ subculture in the twenty-first century. Discovering photography as a teenager, Goldin went on to document the lives of her friends, and her own life, highlighting with breathtaking honesty the joy, love, pain, drug use, and abuse that defined the era. Her exhibition and book *The Ballad of Sexual Dependency* (1986), held up a mirror to the lives of the LGBTQ community in the 1980s, as AIDS overwhelmed New York City, and approached the politics of gender with startling intimacy. Goldin closed the book with the statement: "The book is now a volume of loss, while still a ballad of love." She is now one of the most celebrated contemporary photographers in the world, with her more recent work such as 2010's *Positive Grid* challenging the media representation of HIV-positive individuals.

Opposite: Artist Keith Haring, whose graffiti-inspired art became world-famous and won him fans from Warhol to Madonna. Haring was active in ACT UP before his death from AIDS-related illnesses in 1990.

The first drug treatment for F
zidovudine, also known as AZT
drugs known as nucleoside anal
(NRTIs) that aim to stop HIV fro
it is toxic, and the majority of pe
better understanding of how HI
infection and when a person bec
dormant, as was once thought, b
times. This replication meant dru
treatment to eventually fail.

In 1995 scientists developed a r
inhibitors, which prevent HIV fr
that using more than one drug w
replication and therefore the app
of the virus. Combivir, two drugs
combination therapy was introdu
HIV in people's blood and restori

Although it was hailed as the e
so simple. Antiretroviral therapy
medication, HIV will attack the ir
a treatment option only for those
it, or live in a country that provid

However, over the past 20 years,
the lives of many people with HIV,

Advances have continued. A cou
to 72 hours after exposure, known
highly effective in stopping the vir
development took place: PrEP (pre-
in the US by the FDA. PrEP is a dru
negative people, is highly likely to p

CONTEMPORARY PRIZEWINNERS: CHARLOTTE PRODGER

Charlotte Prodger won the prestigious Turner Prize in 2018 with her solo exhibition *BRIDGIT/Stoneymollan Trail* at Bergen Kunsthall (2017). Working predominantly with moving image and exploring the relationship between the body, identity, and the landscape from a queer perspective, Prodger told *Frieze* in 2014, "Provincial and rural queer narratives feel important to me ... as subjectivities that exist outside the liberal urban context."

NAN GOLDIN
AMERICAN PHOTOGRAPHER

PROFILE OF HER FRIEND DAVID
ARMSTRONG (1954–2014)

David was the first person I ever photographed. He taught me to laugh and named me Nan. I recognized his closet and showed him the way out. We were two hippie kids. David was 14. I was 15. It was 1969 in suburbia.

He appeared like an angel. He showed up at my hippie free school, Satya Community School, a concept of education popular in those days. He was flawless, totally androgynous, with the grace of a young fawn. He looked like an Aubrey Beardsley drawing, with his swanlike hands. I longed to know him.

I hadn't spoken louder than a whisper in over a year, but I had his interest. My reputation preceded me—I had attained legendary status at his former high school when I was thrown out for dealing pot in the parking lot. Somehow he saw me as sophisticated and glamorous. He thought I embodied the promise of what he wanted.

Our first contact was during a school trip to our place in the country called a Thousand Acres. We met in the meat department of the local supermarket, where we were both shoplifting steaks. He turned his light on me and he brought me to life. That intense focus of his curiosity was a gift that everyone who received, competed jealously for the rest of his life. I became the person I wanted to be when I was with David. We were able to fill in the gaps missing in the other. We became inseparable.

I had already discovered my intense attraction to gay men at 13. One of my former boarding schools had been directed by a gay man, his mother and his two dogs. This was a period of such overriding homophobic repression that it became devouring, fed itself, and multiplied like a virus. I'd traveled with the director, Dr. B, and his lover, my boyfriend the West Indian cook, to Europe's cruising grounds and drag bars. So when I met David I sensed he might be gay even before he was in on it.

One night soon after we met, I brought him to my brother's Harvard dorm, where I was staying between foster families. When I crawled into the single bed with him, hoping to seduce him, he moved onto the floor. I asked him if he was afraid I'd rape him and then if he was gay. My saying those words out loud was a moment of liberation for him. Until then he had only allowed himself to acknowledge that he had bisexual fantasies. He credited me with giving him permission to be who he was. I was thrilled.

We hit the ground running and spent the rest of the night cruising Harvard Square. David was a magnet to older men even from the start. He drove men to despair. One divorced his wife before he realized David was a boy. In those years, there was

no open acknowledgment of homosexual people or identity in public. It was all shadows and innuendos.

David was an anachronism in suburbia. He was singular in his androgyny. With his long hair and pierced ears, he caused quite a stir at Dunkin' Donuts. His was not an accepted state of being then. He had searched his whole life in literature and in the culture around us for something that mirrored his desire and source of inexplicable longing. I combed through psychology books for some definition or validation of my own intense attraction to gay men and drag queens—the best out there were books of shame like *Tea and Sympathy*, *The Well of Loneliness*, and *Peyton Place*. We read Diane di Prima's *Miss High Heels* out loud to each other, aroused by her erotic fantasies of long satin gloves on naked flesh. We looked for a subtle indication everywhere, of coded gay undertones, in all the films and books we devoured.

We went to triple features of Fellini, Visconti, and the 30s and 40s Hollywood Goddesses. We devoured Oscar Wilde and Gertrude Stein, the Italian Renaissance, Caravaggio, and dreamt of Warhol's studio. We were proud of being dedicated dilettantes. We envisioned a world of completely fluid sexuality and gender.

David left school and moved into a commune called Wasted Lives for Peace. We lost touch. It was his first time being with other openly gay boys and lesbians. He flourished. He hitchhiked with them to San Francisco for the first Gay Liberation march, the precursor to Gay Pride. He got a job at a store in Harvard Square called the Sphinx. In the front were occult books and in the back, where David was, were antique clothes. He was exquisite, selling tulle and taffeta while lounging like an odalisque on the top of an antique trunk. He started doing semi, then full, drag.

We met up again in 1972 at the Other Side, the underground drag bar in Bay Village. We moved in together with David's first boyfriend Tommy, my first girlfriend Marcy, and two of the queens I was most obsessed with. It was a period of great fluidity and quick changes, Quaaludes and black beauties, sharing friends, clothes, finances, drugs, and occasionally lovers. We lived lifetimes in those short years. It was magical, until my ex-boyfriend burned down our apartment.

Opposite: *Tommy's hand on David's ass on Cambridge Street, Boston.*
Nan Goldin, 1973.

Overleaf: *David and Naomi on the dance floor, The Other Side, Boston..*
Nan Goldin, 1973.

1999

South Africa's first out member of parliament was Mike Waters, appointed in 1999.

1999

The world's first out transgender mayor and then member of parliament Georgina Beyer, of European and Maori descent, served in New Zealand's parliament between 1999 and 2007.

2002

In the UK, the first Conservative MP to come out was Alan Duncan.

2006

Daniele Capezzone was the first bisexual Italian MP to come out.

2006

Italy elected its—and Europe's—first out transgender MP, Vladimir Luxuria.

2009

Brit Nikki Sinclaire was elected as member of the European parliament for the West Midlands, becoming the UK's first openly transgender MEP.

2009

Jóhanna Sigurðardóttir was the first out LGBTQ person to lead a government, serving as prime minister of Iceland between 2009 and 2013.

2011

Anna Grodzka was the first openly transgender politician elected to the Polish parliament.

2011

The second out LGBTQ person to lead a government was Elio Di Rupo, prime minister of Belgium, who held office from 2011 to 2014.

2012

In the US, Stacie Laughton was the first out transgender person to be elected to a state House of Representatives (for New Hampshire) but did not take her seat.

Right above: New Zealand Labor MP Georgina Beyer speaking in favor of the Civil Union Bill, 2004.

Right below: Icelandic Prime Minister Jóhanna Sigurðardóttir celebrating her election, 2009.

Opposite top left: South African MP Zakhele Njabulo Mbhele, 2015.

Opposite top right: Geraldine Roman meeting voters during her successful campaign to become a legislator, Bataan, Philippines, 2016.

Opposite below left: Andrea Jenkins reacting to the news of Melvin Carter's election win in Minnesota, USA, 2017.

Opposite below right: Leo Varadkar, Irish Prime Minister, at the Dublin Pride Parade in 2015.

2013

The third out LGBTQ person to lead a government was Xavier Bettel, who became Luxembourg's prime minister in 2013 and, as of early 2019, is still in office.

2014

Zakhele Mbhele became South Africa's first openly gay Black member of parliament.

2016

The Philippines elected its first transgender politician, Geraldine Roman, to Congress.

2016

In Sri Lanka, Niluka Ekanayake became governor of Central Province, and the first transgender woman to hold the post of governor.

2016

Audrey Tang was invited to be minister without portfolio in Taiwan's Executive Yuan, making her the first trans person to be made a member of cabinet.

2017

In 2017, Danica Roem was elected to the Virginia House of Delegates, becoming the first openly transgender politician in the US to take her seat.

2017

Andrea Jenkins became the first openly transgender Black woman elected to public office in the US.

2018

Latvia elected two openly LGBTQ MPs for the first time, Edgars Rinkēvičs and Marija Golubeva.

2018

Colorado elected Democrat Jared Polis in the midterms, making him the first openly gay governor in the US.

2019

Sharice Davids became Kansas' first LGBTQ congressmember, and the first gay Native American woman politician.

homosexuality as an illness in 1990, but acceptance by the general public would by no means immediately follow this development.

In 1990, the year after Stonewall's formation, actor Michael Boothe was beaten to death by a group of six men in a public toilet near Elthorne Park, west London. In the year before, there had been several cases of gay men stabbed or battered to death which were not adequately investigated by the undoubtedly institutionally homophobic police. The London gay community were outraged. Concerned that the murders of cottaging gay men would not be prioritized by a mainstream movement, activists Simon Watney, Chris Woods, Keith Alcorn, and Peter Tatchell organized a public meeting days after Boothe's death, to create an angrier, more confrontational group. The first public action by OutRage! was a demonstration at the public toilets in Hyde Park on June 7, 1990, in protest of the Metropolitan Police's policy of sending "pretty policemen"— handsome undercover officers—into public restrooms to entrap gay men. While Stonewall lobbied politicians and sympathetic journalists, OutRage! continued its protests and displays of provocative banners, such as one protesting Defence Secretary Michael Portillo's decision to uphold the military's ban on LGBT personnel, with the slogan "Portillo screws queer soldiers!"

Also formed in 1990, in New York City, was direct action group Queer Nation. The word "queer" had long seen use as a slur; Queer Nation is responsible for starting the term's reclamation. By now, the word has

Opposite: Peter Tatchell (center) protesting with OutRage! in Parliament Square at London's 1996 Pride Festival. Michael Portillo, Secretary of State for Defence at the time, upheld the ban on openly LGBT people serving in the UK military. Years later, Portillo confirmed rumors that he had had homosexual encounters.

Top: Ian McKellen leaving 10 Downing Street after talks with Prime Minister John Major in 1991. John Major later said that he "learned a great deal" about gay people and their rights during this meeting.

Right: Kyle Minogue performs with Elton John, in drag, at the 1995 Stonewall Equality Show at the Royal Albert Hall, London. They performed the duet "Sisters."

DAVID FURNISH
CHAIR OF THE ELTON JOHN AIDS FOUNDATION. FOUNDED IN 1992, THE EJAF HAS RAISED OVER $400 MILLION FOR HIV-RELATED PROGRAMS.

The story of HIV and AIDS today is essentially a good news one. We're now in a position where, if everybody knew their HIV status and had access to anti-retroviral medication, we would have no new infections.

PrEP means that if you are HIV-negative and taking the medication as advised, you will reduce your risk of HIV infection by 95%.

If you have HIV and you know your status, and you are adhering to anti-retroviral treatment as directed by your physician, then in almost every instance people's viral loads go down to zero. When that happens, even though you are HIV-positive, you cannot pass the virus on. That's pretty major.

There are two major challenges. There is still stigma, which is a hangover from when AIDS was a disease of shame and death, and considered to be only something caught by gay people, intravenous drug users, or the "sexually promiscuous," all of whom were highly shamed groups.

The other challenge is about access to medication. In America, we're seeing the highest incidence of new infections in the Deep South amongst African American gay and bisexual men, because they have a double dose of homophobia from within their own community and often a complete lack of access to any healthcare whatsoever.

I've seen the situation change so much. Back in the early nineties, I remember going to Kenya and South Africa, and there was nothing we could do other than offer palliative care. Sometimes we'd go to visit a person and they'd die before we arrived. There were caskets everywhere. You could sense death everywhere. People were ashamed. Today we see people wearing "I'm HIV positive" T-shirts, showing that, with education, we can turn HIV from a badge of shame to a badge of courage.

The Reagan and Bush Sr. administrations turned a blind eye to HIV and AIDS because it was "a gay disease" and nobody cared, and it went on to become the biggest disease affecting the world today. Seventy million infections, 37 million deaths. What we have seen unequivocally, in countries where it is illegal to be gay or that are deeply homophobic, is that HIV becomes even more stigmatized and people end up not wanting to test, or pick up medication, for fear of being associated with "that gay disease." That results in new HIV infections across all of society. The same with sex workers and IV-drug users. If we make judgments, we're never going to stop this disease. If we get to those people, with information and access to testing and treatment and needle exchanges, we would stop those new infections. Sex is a fact in our society. Addiction is a fact in our society. The days of Nancy Reagan saying "Just say no" are over.

Another major problem is that in some parts of the world, the medications are ridiculously expensive. One prescription of PrEP in America, outside of health insurance, is around $4,300. If you have health insurance, it will cover the cost or PrEP, but if you are a poor African American man in the South, you likely won't have any health insurance, and buying PrEP is completely out of your reach.

The revolutionary thing President Clinton did regarding Africa, when medicines were priced way beyond the capabilities of the healthcare systems of those countries, was that he went to the drug companies and said we need to get people medication. He galvanized the use of the generic drugs to be provided at a fraction of the cost. We need that now.

Deaths now from AIDS are mostly when HIV has been diagnosed a long time after a person has contracted it, and it's been untreated. So the sooner we know, the sooner we get people on treatment—and people must adhere to the treatment; you can't stop it and start it; and that means being able to continue to afford it—then the news has never been better. Your life expectancy is the same as someone who is HIV-negative. The MP in British Parliament, Lloyd Russell-Moyle, who came out about his status, right the way back to Magic Johnson coming out about his—there's a history of bravery and we need more people to say, "I live with this disease and I live a full life and now I'm on medication; I cannot pass the virus on to anyone else." We have to continue to take the shame out of it.

I'm proud of what the Elton John AIDS foundation has done. We started in the US in 1992 and the UK in 1993, and we have raised more than $400 million in the last 25 years and funded thousands of schemes to help people living with HIV and to reduce stigma. In Britain, we funded the legal challenge to the NHS which enabled the NHS trial. We also funded PrepSter, which helps men purchase legitimate generic PrEP drugs from abroad. That's resulted in a dramatic turnaround in new infections. We won't be happy until there are no new infections. It is possible if we know the facts, remove the stigma, know our status, and everyone has access to medication.

Opposite: David Furnish and his now-husband Sir Elton John, visiting the AIDS Memorial Quilt during its display on the National Mall in Washington, DC, during the nineteenth International AIDS Conference, July 2012.

CULTURE: MOVIES

German activist Magnus Hirschfeld co-wrote what is now considered the world's first explicitly pro-gay film. *Different From The Others* (1919) recounts the love affair of two musicians, doomed by the repressive times. Later, after Hollywood's infamous Hays Code of self-censorship was dropped in 1968, the first American film to examine gay lives was *The Boys in the Band* (1970), a film of Mart Crowley's hit play. Though a painful depiction of self-loathing, it was not as bleak as the psychopathic homosexual trope that the Code had facilitated by allowing only negative portrayals of "sex perversion." The following five decades saw some incredible successes and failures in the portrayal of LGBTQ lives on screen.

1970s

In the years after the Stonewall riots, gay directors and writers were beginning to tell the stories of LGBTQ lives. John Schlesinger directed gay and bisexual characters in *Midnight Cowboy* (1969) and *Sunday Bloody Sunday* (1971), and in 1972 the musical *Cabaret*, based on a novel by Christopher Isherwood and featuring a bisexual protagonist, became a huge hit, winning eight Oscars. Filmmakers such as James Bidgood (*Pink Narcissus*, 1971), Chantal Akerman (*Je Tu Il Elle*, 1974), Jan Oxenberg (*A Comedy in Six Unnatural Acts*, 1975), Derek Jarman (*Sebastiane*, 1976), and Rainer Werner Fassbinder (*The Bitter Tears of Petra Von Kant*, 1972) all made an impact. Trans lives featured in the Warhol-produced *Women In Revolt* (1971) and Fassbinder's *In a Year of 13 Moons* (1978), and the mainstream thriller *Dog Day Afternoon* (1975) included a trans woman character played by actor Chris Sarandon.

Then in 1972, the first TV movie to portray homosexuality with tenderness was screened: *That Certain Summer*, about a father coming out to his teenage son.

Commenting in 2007 on the fact that he'd been advised not to take the part, one of the lead (heterosexual) actors, Martin Sheen, said, "I'd robbed banks and kidnapped children and raped women and murdered people, you know, in any number of shows. Now I was going to play a gay guy and that was like considered a career ender. Oh, for Christ's sake! What kind of culture do we live in?"

The British film *Nighthawks* (1978) explored a gay man's life in London. *La Cage aux Folles*—a comedy centered on a gay couple who run a nightclub—was the second-highest grossing film of 1978 in France, and remains one of the most successful ever foreign-language films in the US.

Above: The cast of the film adaptation of Broadway classic *Boys in the Band*, by Mart Crowley, directed by William Friedkin, 1970.

1980s

Mainstream audiences continued to be exposed to negative tropes about the LGBTQ community. In 1980 both *Cruising*, starring Al Pacino, about a serial killer targeting men on the leather scene, and *Windows*, about a lesbian stalker ("Somebody loves Emily . . . too much"), provoked demonstrations. LGBTQ audiences were subjected to insults at the cinema on a regular basis—*Teen Wolf* (1985) is a prime example of Hollywood's casual homophobia. "If you're gonna tell me you're a fag, I don't think I can handle it," says a character to his buddy, played by Michael J. Fox, who replies, offended, "I'm not a fag, I'm a werewolf!"

The glimmers of positivity were just that—glimmers. *Desert Hearts* (1985) was a breakthrough for lesbian representation, but *The Color Purple* (1985) and *Fried Green Tomatoes* (1991) both watered down the themes of the novels on which they are based., turning lesbian couples into platonic friends.

An Early Frost (1985), *Parting Glances* (1986), and *Longtime Companion* (1989) all addressed AIDS, but none were mainstream hits. The game-changing *Philadelphia* (1993) featured two of the world's biggest stars: Tom Hanks, who is fired when his bosses find out he has AIDS, and Denzel Washington, the lawyer who takes his case.

Arthouse flicks *My Beautiful Laundrette* (1985), *Maurice* (1987), *Torch Song Trilogy* (1988), and *Kiss of the Spider Woman* (1985) were all successes, the latter winning William Hurt the Best Actor Oscar—which provoked anger in some quarters, considering so many gay actors were closeted, or like Harvey Fierstein (both writer and star of *Torch Song Trilogy*), overlooked. In 1989, *Looking for Langston* explored black gay experience in New York's Harlem Renaissance in the 1920s.

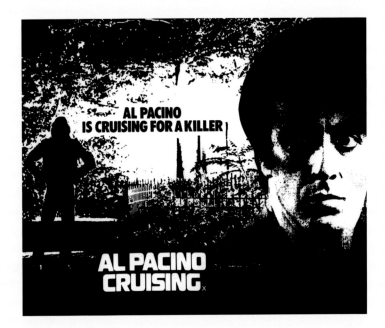

Above: What a difference a decade makes. The poster for William Friedkin's next film about gay men after 1970's *The Boys in the Band* was the horrific *Cruising* (1980), starring Al Pacino as a man tracking a killer on New York's leather scene.

Below: Helen Shaver, Patricia Charbonneau, and Audra Lindley starred in a rare (for the time) positive portrayal of lesbians in 1985's classic *Desert Hearts,* based on the Jane Rule novel *Desert of the Heart.*

TEN GREAT TRANS FILMS

Different for Girls (1996)
Ma Vie en Rose (1997)
Breakfast on Pluto (2005)
Transamerica (2005, documentary)
Becoming Chaz (2011)

Gun Hill Road (2011)
Boy Meets Girl (2014)
Drunktown's Finest (2014)
Tangerine (2015)
A Fantastic Woman (2017)

TEN MOVIES WITH LGBTQ CHARACTERS OF COLOR

Paris is Burning (1990, documentary)
The Watermelon Woman (1996)
*Still Black: A Portrait of Black
   Transmen* (2008, documentary)
Circumstance (2011)
Pariah (2011)

My Brother the Devil (2012)
Call Me Kuchu (2012, documentary)
The Skinny (2012)
Blackbird (2014)
Moonlight (2016)

TEN FEELGOOD FILMS FOR GAY GUYS

Beautiful Thing (1996)
Big Eden (2000)
Kinky Boots (2005)
Weekend (2011)
Pride (2014)
Brother to Brother (2014)
The Way He Looks (2014)
Strike a Pose (2016, documentary)
God's Own Country (2017)
Love, Simon (2018)

TEN FEELGOOD FILMS FOR LESBIANS

*The Incredibly True Adventure of Two Girls
   in Love* (1995)
Show Me Love (1998)
But I'm a Cheerleader (1999)
Kissing Jessica Stein (2001)
D.E.B.S. (2004)
Saving Face (2004)
I Can't Think Straight (2008)
The Kids Are All Right (2010)
Mosquita y Mari (2012)
Hearts Beat Loud (2018)

PEDRO ALMODÓVAR

The Spanish filmmaker created his own genre of blackly comedic drama, often with LGBTQ themes, which gained respect in the mainstream. Usually with strong female characters and often with sympathetic or empowered trans characters, his notable films include his breakout *Women On The Verge of A Nervous Breakdown* (1988), which was nominated for the Best Foreign Language Academy Award, and *All About My Mother* (1999) which won in that category at the Academy Awards, the Golden Globes and the BAFTAs, *Bad Education* (2004) and *The Skin I Live In* (2011).

DEREK JARMAN

Multi-disciplinary artist Jarman was an activist and revolutionary, an anarchic anti-establishment voice in Britain from the 1970s until his death from an AIDS-related illness in 1994. His first full-length film, *Sebastiane* (1976), is considered to be the first pro-gay British film, and was met with huge controversy when it was screened on national television. One of the most outspoken opponents of Section 28 and the Thatcher government, his works include *Jubilee* (1978), *Caravaggio* (1986), *The Last of England* (1987), and *Blue* (1993).

ARTHOUSE LGBTQ FILMS WORLDWIDE

The Wedding Banquet (Taiwan, 1993)
Heavenly Creatures (New Zealand, 1994)
The Celluloid Closet (US, 1995, documentary)
À Toute Vitesse (France, 1996)
Lilies (Canada, 1996)
Priest (UK, 1996)
Regular Guys (Germany, 1996)
Bent (UK, 1997)
Happy Together (Hong Kong, 1997)

Wilde (UK, 1997)
From the Edge of the City (Greece, 1998)
Get Real (UK, 1998)
High Art (Canada/US, 1998)
Man Is a Woman (France, 1998)
Show Me Love (Sweden, 1998)
The Trio (Germany, 1998)
Beau Travail (France, 1999)
Before Night Falls (US, 2000)
Drôle de Félix (France, 2000)

TEN FILMS FOR BISEXUALS

Henry & June (1990)
Frieda (2002)
Star Appeal (2004)
Imagine Me & You (2005)
Rent (2005)
City Without Baseball (2008)
Margarita with a Straw (2014)
Appropriate Behavior (2014)
Atomic Blonde (2017)
Bohemian Rhapsody (2018)

Top: Oscar-winning 1999 Spanish film *Todo Sobre Mi Madre* (*All About My Mother*).

Above: Revolutionary filmmaker, artist and activist Derek Jarman (middle), at an OutRage! protest, 1991.

Opposite top: Georges Du Fresne as a transgender teenager in the 1997 film *Ma Vie en Rose*, directed by Alain Berliner.

Opposite below: Leslie Cheung and Tony Leung Chiu-wai in the 1997 film *Happy Together*, directed by Wong Kar-wai.

Overleaf: Chiron (Trevante Rhodes) expresses intimacy to Kevin (André Holland) in the stunning smash hit film *Moonlight* (2016), which won Best Picture, Best Supporting Actor and Best Adapted Screenplay at the 2017 Academy Awards.

LESBIAN AVENGERS

Stormé DeLarverie was born on Christmas Eve, 1920, in New Orleans, the daughter of a white man and a black woman. With her striking, statuesque look, she performed as the drag king MC of the Jewel Box Revue, a drag show that toured America from 1955 to 1969. DeLarverie was at the Stonewall Inn on the night of the riots. It's never been certain who started them, but many have said it was a butch lesbian. Some claimed it was DeLarverie, and she agreed.

A cop said to me, 'Move, faggot', thinking that I was a gay guy," she said in an interview, "I said, 'I will not! And don't you dare touch me.' With that, the cop shoved me and I instinctively punched him right in his face. He bled! He was then dropping to the ground—not me."

Her partner of 25 years, Diana, died in the 1970s. In later years, DeLarverie was respected as a Stonewall veteran and worked as a doorperson at various lesbian bars, including the Cubbyhole, and would patrol the Greenwich Village area, checking in on venues to make sure there was no "ugliness" of any kind. Many refer to DeLarverie as the "lesbian Rosa Parks," and she has become a powerful symbol of lesbian pride and power, but also of the erasure from mainstream LGBTQ history of African Americans and the gender-nonconforming.

The role of gay men and gay organizations in the LGBTQ rights movement has, in the telling of its history, tended to be given prominence over others. Lesbians have had to deal with the intersection of homophobia and sexism, both from outside the LGBTQ community and sometimes from within it. However, many lesbian-specific organizations have overcome this prejudice to become icons of the movement, and in fact are at the heart of it. The organization Dykes on Bikes was formed in 1976 by a group of founding members, including Soni Wolf, and saw lesbians on motorcycles lead the San Francisco Pride Parade. The contingent has become a popular (controversial to some, due to their name) part of many Pride marches across the world, from Europe and Canada to Australia and Israel. The lesbian feminist movement formed during the 1970s and 1980s, was highly critical of heteronormativity and male supremacy, and became a linchpin of modern feminism.

While much has been written about the apparent divisions between the gay and lesbian contingents of the LGBTQ equality movement, it's less well-publicized that lesbians were at the forefront of the response to the AIDS crisis, nursing their gay brothers, and protesting Section 28, as previously mentioned.

Right above: Lesbians of color march at the Los Angeles Pride parade, 1979.

Right: A couple in tuxedos at the Second National March on Washington for Lesbian and Gay Rights, 1987.

Opposite: Stormé DeLarverie, believed to be the lesbian at the Stonewall riots who fought back against the police, asked for help, and inspired the first stone to be thrown at a police van. Pictured in New York, 1986.

In New York in 1992, the Lesbian Avengers, a group focused on increasing lesbian survival and visibility, was formed. They staged actions and campaigns, protesting misogyny, homophobic school curricula, and homophobia in politics. One of the group's highest-profile achievements was the organization of the first official Dyke March, which was preceded by two similar events. In May 1981, in Vancouver, Canada, 200 lesbians held a march outside a lesbian conference. In October, Lesbians Against the Right did the same in Toronto, Canada. The first official Dyke March, of over 20,000 lesbians took place on April 24, 1993, the day before the historic March on Washington for Lesbian, Gay, and Bi Equal Rights and Liberation—at which over a million LGBTQ people protested inequality. Since this inaugural event, more and more Dyke Marches have sprung up across the globe, usually taking place just before the Gay Pride events.

Despite the continuing dominance of gay men in the LGBTQ narrative, there are an increasing number of high-profile out women, including, in the UK, TV presenters Sandi Toksvig, Sue Perkins, and Clare Balding, Olympic boxer Nicola Adams, leading politicians Ruth Davidson and Angela Eagle, former Stonewall Chief Executive Ruth Hunt, and actor and model Cara Delevingne. In Spain, politician Ángeles Álvarez campaigns against gender violence, and actor and former Miss Spain

Patricia Yurena is the first out national beauty queen in the world. In France, former world number one tennis player Amélie Mauresmo came out aged 19 in 1999, while singer-songwriter Héloïse Letissier, aka Christine and the Queens, who identifies as pansexual, shot to fame with the release of her debut album in 2014. Belgian filmmaker Chantal Akerman, who preferred not to be defined by her sexuality, was hailed as a pioneer for her art house masterpiece *Jeanne Dielman, 23 Quai du Commerce, 1080 Bruxelles*.

The US is home to influential out women, including sports icon Martina Navratilova, singer Melissa Etheridge, actors Jodie Foster, Sarah Paulson, and Jane Lynch, comedian Wanda Sykes, TV presenters Rachel Maddow and Robin Roberts and, of course, arguably the most influential LGBTQ person in the world, Ellen DeGeneres.

Above: The Lesbian Avengers protest at the White House during the Gay Rights March in April, 1993. Over a million LGBTQ activists and their families participated in what was then the largest gathering of the LGBTQ community in history.

Opposite: A protester carrying one of the many signs displayed at 1993's record-breaking Gay Rights March in Washington, DC.

ALLIES

FRIENDS AND FAMILY

In 1968, young gay student Morty Manford was one of the founder members of the student group Gay People at Colombia University. Four years later, by then a Stonewall Riots veteran, he was ejected and brutally attacked after distributing flyers at a political dinner.

When his mother Jeanne heard, she wrote an angry letter to the *New York Post*. In 1972, when people were mostly ashamed of having gay kids, this was radical. Jeanne marched with her son in that June's pride parade, carrying a sign saying, "Parents of Gays: Unite in Support for Our Children." Overwhelmed by the reception, she later said, "Young people were hugging me, kissing me, screaming, asking if I would talk to their parents." So Jeanne and her husband Jules decided to start a group, as she said, to "build a bridge between the gay and the heterosexual community." The group was called Parents of Gays and, at its first meeting, attracted 20 people.

Morty became an assistant New York State attorney general and pushed through a key gay rights law in 1986. He died from AIDS-related illnesses in May 1992, aged 41. Jeanne lived to the age of 92 and died in 2013, but today her group, later renamed Parents, Families and Friends of Lesbians and Gays (and now simply PFLAG), is America's biggest organization for families of LGBTQ people, and has kept countless parents united with their children. Affiliate groups run in 15 countries, including the UK, China, Latin America, and Israel.

Jeanne symbolizes a vitally important group that is sometimes overlooked: allies. Both Sir John Wolfenden and Leo Abse MP, who pushed John Wolfenden's recommendations into law, were heterosexual. In the UK, the Albert Kennedy Trust was started by a heterosexual foster-care professional called Cath Hall, after the death in 1989 of a young man in the care system who fell to his death from the roof of a multistory parking garage. Many straight people, though not as many as we would have liked, have been of vital help and support over the last five decades.

Hollywood celebrities were among the first to respond to the AIDS crisis. Elizabeth Taylor organized the first AIDS Project Los Angeles fundraiser and used her own money to start the Elizabeth Taylor AIDS Foundation. She worked tirelessly, shaming three presidents for not doing enough to combat AIDS and forcing Reagan to speak

publicly about the disease for the first time. Carrie Fisher, Joan Rivers, Liza Minnelli, Sharon Stone, and Bette Midler were among those who first rallied. Performing at the 1991 AIDS Benefit Los Angeles, Midler said, "I didn't start running for the hills like a lot of people did. Nearly everyone I started out with has died."

Princess Diana's advocacy of gay rights led to *The Mail on Sunday*'s John Junor to label her "the patron saint of sodomy."

Richard Gere, who has a gay brother, starred in *Bent* in 1979. Madonna, with a gay brother, and gay best friends who died of

Right: Jeanne Manford and her son, gay activist Morty Manford, march in the 1972 Christopher Street Liberation Day March, the precursor to what is now known as NY Pride. From this moment grew PFLAG, the first and largest organization for lesbian, gay, bisexual, transgender, and queer (LGBTQ) people, their parents and families, and allies.

Opposite: Bette Midler, pictured here playing at the Continental Baths, a gay bathhouse in New York City, 1972, was one of the earliest celebrity supporters of people with HIV and AIDS.

AIDS, broke cultural boundaries by pushing gay culture into the mainstream, portraying same-sex themes in her work and speaking out about homophobia.

While many celebrities have paid lip service to their gay fan bases since these pioneers, others walk the walk. Kylie Minogue was one of the first to play gay clubs and benefits, while in recent years, Cyndi Lauper founded a major charity to support LGBTQ youth. Ariana Grande is also vocally supportive of her gay fan base, as is British band Little Mix.

Oprah Winfrey frequently discussed LGBTQ issues on her show and played Ellen DeGeneres' therapist when she came out on her sitcom *Ellen*. The UK's Channel 4 has, from its inception in 1982, been gay-friendly, airing gay work and commissioning the original series of *Queer As Folk*. *Golden Girls* actor Bea Arthur became a passionate advocate for LGBTQ homeless youth and Daniel Radcliffe has made public service announcements for the Trevor Project.

Rap singer Macklemore performed his same-sex marriage anthem,

"Same Love," during the 2014 Grammys, where various couples were married by Queen Latifah, with Madonna as the wedding singer, and again at the Australian National Rugby League final in 2017, during ferocious campaigning ahead of the country's same-sex marriage referendum.

Other supportive celebrities with LGBTQ siblings include:	Celebrities with LGBTQ children include:
Garth Brooks	Warren Beatty and Annette Bening
Madonna	Jackie Chan
Lena Dunham	Dick Cheney
Chris Evans	Cher
Colin Farrell	Sally Field
Ariana Grande	Magic Johnson
Anne Hathaway	Anne Rice
Adam Levine	Cybil Shepherd
Marlee Martin	Barbra Streisand
Kevin Smith	Isiah Thomas
Patricia, Rosanna, and David	Gloria Vanderbilt
Arquette	Alice Walker

Above: Madonna has always been one of the biggest celebrity allies, using her immense fame to speak out against homophobia and including LGBTQ imagery in her work. *Madonna: Truth or Dare*, the 1991 film documenting her Blond Ambition tour, opened up gay culture to her fans, as many of her close-knit group of backing dancers on the tour (pictured) were gay.

Opposite: With a lesbian sister, singer Cyndi Lauper has been one of showbusiness's biggest allies, starting her own True Colors foundation for homeless LGBTQ kids and writing the musical *Kinky Boots*. Here, she is pictured during the Closing Ceremony of the Gay Games VII in Chicago, 2006.

CULTURE: TELEVISION

The first gay characters on American television were brief appearances from peripheral characters, and always met with controversy. Heterosexual TV producer Norman Lear deserves credit for including the first gay character on US television—a one-episode character called Steve in popular 1971 sitcom *All in the Family*, and perhaps the first gay couple in the short-lived 1975 sitcom *Hot L Baltimore*. The first trans character, a doctor who transitions to female, was introduced the same year on CBS's *Medical Center*.

The 1972 ABC sitcom *The Corner Bar* was the first to feature a recurrent gay character, a set designer called Peter—but the character was condemned as a stereotype and the jokes as homophobic by the Gay Activists Alliance. The TV film *That Certain Summer* with Martin Sheen and Hal Holbrook was better received, gaining six Emmy nominations and winning one. In 1977 ABC featured Billy Crystal as a recurring gay character called Jodie Dallas in its controversial adult-themed sitcom *Soap*, which aired until 1981.

From the 1970s on, British TV slowly began to take notice of LGBTQ lives, airing *A Change of Sex*, a series of three documentaries about transitioning trans woman Julia Grant, another about trans lives called *What Am I?*, and an ITV documentary about gay men, *Male Sexuality*. But it was soaps that would make the most impact.

Acclaimed for bringing serious social issues to children's drama *Grange Hill*, writer-producer Phil Redmond brought the first gay character to British soap opera in 1982: Gordon Collins, in Channel 4's *Brookside*. In

1994 *Brookside*'s Beth Jordache, played by Anna Friel, realized she was gay with a sensational kiss that left the media torn between outrage and titillation—it was the first pre-9 p.m. watershed lesbian kiss on British TV.

EastEnders, the wildly popular UK soap created by producer Julia Smith and gay writer Tony Holland in 1985, was met with the *Sun* headline "EASTBENDERS!" when the soap introduced its first gay character in 1986: Colin Russell, played by Michael Cashman. But despite such sensationalist headlines from the tabloids, the positive impact of having a gay man in the nation's homes twice a week was huge.

While British soaps made headway, LGBTQ representation on US television was not making so much progress. From its first episode in 1981, glamorous mega-soap *Dynasty* featured gay character Steven Carrington, often cited as the first gay character in a primetime show, but producers kept having him sleep with women, something that caused the original actor to leave the show. Steven returned two seasons later played by a new actor—his new face was explained away by a fire on an oil rig.

One of the most groundbreaking TV series in terms of representation was *Roseanne*, Roseanne Barr's smash-hit sitcom that originally ran from 1988 till 1997 and featured the gay characters Leon, Roseanne's boss, and family friend Nancy, played by Sandra Bernhard. The show was intelligent: it showed Roseanne organizing male strippers, pink triangle banners, and flamingos for Leon's wedding—to which he objected. In 1993, the Channel 4 and PBS adaptation of Armistead Maupin's *Tales of the City*, featuring gay, bisexual, and trans central characters, was a major moment for LGBTQ television (the new series aired on Netflix in 2019,

starring Laura Linney, Olympia Dukakis, and Ellen Page).

During the 1990s, producers included gay characters—although they were most often on the periphery—in many of the biggest shows in the US, including *Hill Street Blues*, *ER*, *LA Law*, and *My So-Called Life*.

A watershed moment occurred in 1997 when Ellen DeGeneres, star of hit sitcom *Ellen*, and her eponymous character both came out. In 1997 ABC recorded the (codenamed) "Puppy Episode," in which Ellen's crush on a character played by Laura Dern helps her realize she is gay, something she announces accidentally across an airport public address system. Announced on the cover of *Time* magazine, Ellen's personal and professional coming out was hugely high profile and controversial. Criticized for being "too gay," the show's ratings slowly went down and it was eventually canceled. Nevertheless, a major seal had been broken.

A year later, NBC studios took a chance on a script about a gay lawyer and his female best friend, by gay/straight writer combo Max Mutchnick and David Kohan. Their idea capitalized on the previous year's hit film *My Best Friend's Wedding* with Rupert Everett as Julia Roberts's gay friend, and also believed that *Ellen* spent too much time on gay issues, rather than just focusing on the comedy. Despite getting mixed reviews

Opposite: *Queer As Folk*. After Russell T. Davies's smash hit British show broke new ground and made news across the world, Showtime commissioned an American version that ran from 2000 to 2005 (pictured).

Above: Ellen DeGeneres comes out to Laura Dern on "The Puppy Episode" of her hit show *Ellen*, 1997. The episode caused a public backlash and ratings suffered, eventually resulting in *Ellen*'s cancellation, and damaging Dern's career.

Above: *The L Word* was a huge hit for the Showtime network. It was the first show for and by lesbian women, airing from 2004–09.

Left: The Fab Five, cast of Netflix's 2018 *Queer Eye*, the revamped version of Bravo's *Queer Eye for the Straight Guy*.

Opposite: Trans actor Laverne Cox broke new ground in women's prison drama *Orange is the New Black*, which premiered on Netflix in 2013 and became a huge hit.

initially, *Will & Grace* went on to become a gargantuan mainstream hit and cultural phenomenon. US Vice President Joe Biden would say years later that the show "did more to educate the American public than almost anything anybody has ever done so far."

Over the pond, Channel 4 screened writer Russell T. Davies's bold, unashamed *Queer As Folk*, which was then the most confrontational and unapologetic gay series ever made. It became a hit, and the US version, produced by Showtime, went on to run from 2000 until 2005. Widely regarded as inspired by *Queer As Folk*, *The L Word* ran from 2004 until 2009, marking a huge step forward for lesbian representation—a legacy continued in the 2019 sequel series. As Alison Glock commented in the *New York Times* in 2005, "before *The L Word*, lesbians barely existed in television." By this point, it was becoming normal to include lesbian, gay, and bisexual characters in television programs, but trans audiences were still waiting to be represented on the small screen.

In 2003, cable channel Bravo programmed *Queer Eye for the Straight Guy*, showing five gay men restyling straight guys, playing to the stereotype that gay men were intrinsically more fashionable than straight ones. A cliché, yes, but nevertheless more welcome than the depiction of homosexuals as criminals or victims, which had at one point been the norm. The rebooted *Queer Eye*, streaming on Netflix since 2018, has shifted focus dramatically and has achieved cult status as one of the most heart-warming and tear-jerking shows currently airing. The five new presenters take it upon themselves to show their subjects (a diverse group, from self-described "redneck" Tom to semi-closeted and struggling AJ, along with straight women, lesbians, and a trans man), and the audience, how to be happy as their authentic selves—often with emotional results.

After the success of the second season of *Queer As Folk* and his bisexual drama *Bob and Rose*, the BBC asked Russell T. Davies to head a new era of the cult sci-fi series *Doctor Who*. Davies added queer flourishes and created a post-watershed spin off, *Torchwood*, led by a pansexual, time-traveling alien played by John Barrowman. In 2017, *Doctor Who* would have its first openly gay companion, significant when it is considered primarily a children's program.

Drag legend RuPaul came into his own in 2009 with *RuPaul's Drag Race*, a competitive reality TV show, originally on gay channel Logo. Expected to be nothing but glamor and bitching, it turned out to also be moving and sincere, and depicted many of the issues that femme-presenting queer men can face. By 2019, it had won 9 Emmy Awards and was one of the LGBTQ community's best-loved shows of all time.

In 2013, *Orange is the New Black*, about a diverse group of women in an American prison, premiered. It has gone on to become the most-watched original series on streaming giant Netflix, finally giving Lea DeLaria, the first out comic on US late-night TV, the spotlight she deserved, and making a star out of trans actor Laverne Cox.

The following year, Amazon Studios ran an original series of their own, *Transparent*, created by Jill Soloway, about a family whose father transitions to female. *Transparent* was a hit, engaging with a broader conversation about the acceptance of transgender people, though it faced controversy for casting a cisgender man—one later fired for sexual harassment—as the trans main character. Transgender issues also received massive attention with the coming out of Caitlyn Jenner.

Producer/writer Ryan Murphy has thrust LGBTQ television forward to an incredible degree. From musical sensation *Glee*, to *The Assassination of Gianni Versace*, *The Normal Heart*, and the extraordinary *Pose*—which is set in New York's ballroom scene and features the largest ever cast of trans characters—he has sealed his position as an important gay man in Hollywood history, and in 2018 signed a Netflix deal worth $300 million. The rise of Netflix and other streaming services has proven that there is a huge and diverse audience for such shows.

Online, Italian web series *G&T*, focusing on the developing relationship of childhood friends Giulio and Tommaso, has had more than 91 million views on YouTube, and its many fans have created subtitles for the series in more than 10 languages.

REVEREND TROY PERRY
FOUNDER OF THE LGBTQ-INCLUSIVE
METROPOLITAN COMMUNITY CHURCH

I grew up in Florida and was raised in a southern Baptist background. I was told that God couldn't love me if I was gay and when I came out, at first, I believed that. I thought, "My church tells me God can't love me, so that's that." But I had a call to ministry at a very young age.

When I was 18, I went to my pastor and told him about my "funny feelings," as I called them. I didn't know the word homosexual. He said: "Oh my God, I know what you're trying to tell me. All you need to do is marry a woman, that will take care of that problem"—and I married his daughter. Five years and two children later, we decided to divorce. I kept struggling. I was drafted into the US military and spent two years abroad. When I came home, I fell deeply in love with a man for the first time. It was six of the best/worst months of my life. He wanted to open the relationship up, I didn't, and he walked out of my life. I tried to take my life, but thank God, my roommate broke down the door and took me to the hospital. It was there that an African American nurse said to me, "I don't know why you've done this. It's stupid. I've tried it too." And she said, "Isn't there someone you can talk to? Can't you just look up?" and she pressed a button in me. When I got home I was lying in bed, thinking about what happened the night before, and I felt that joy in my heart. I said "God, you can't love me, I'm still a homosexual, that hasn't changed." Even 50 years later I still remember, God spoke to me in a small still voice and said, "Troy, I love you. And I don't have stepsons and daughters." And with that I knew then that I could be gay and part of the Christian faith.

I started dating again. I was at a dance bar in LA and my date got arrested in the middle of a bar for slapping our friend's butt. Back at my place, he was crying and he told me nobody cared about him. When I said I and God did, he told me that wasn't true and how, when he was 15, he was ordered out of Sunday school because his priest was afraid he would contaminate other kids.

I prayed that night: "Alright God, I think I found my niche. If you want to see a church that has a special outreach into the gay and lesbian community but open to everybody, just tell me when."

And that small, still voice said: "Now."

So I took out an ad in the *Advocate* newspaper. I said "Reverend Troy Perry," gave my home address, October 6, 1968, and 12 people showed up in my living room. We started growing rapidly and within 18 months we had over 1,000 people in attendance and owned our first piece of property.

We believed in Christian social action. We started immediately. We opened food pantries. We fed the hungry, we clothed the naked: we did what Jesus did. I also started leading demonstrations. There was resistance. There were people in the LGBT community who wished I wasn't a clergyperson, but they recognized I had skills and had organized the largest organization at that time. In the larger community, oh my God, everybody immediately piled in: "You can't be a Christian and a homosexual!" I debated everybody and anybody. They were shocked that I loved scripture. They could quote one, I could quote fifteen! I had people spit in my face. I was slapped in the face, I had people who tried to murder me. I went through all that. But I was also invited to the White House to talk about gay rights.

Bill Clinton was very good to me. I was a delegate on hate crimes, was invited to the first White House conference on AIDS, I had breakfast with President Clinton and Vice President Gore. My partner and I were invited by President Obama to the White House fortieth anniversary celebration of the Stonewall Riots. I've been honored, but I have had people try to do all kinds of things. One of our churches was burnt down to the ground, eight of our pastors were murdered.

Today, a large segment of the Christian Church is now welcoming. The Metropolitan Community Church, and people like me who met them and talked to them, really challenged them. The United Methodist Church, Pentecostals, and the Southern Baptist Convention still teach that homosexuality is not compatible with the gospel. The United Church of Christ accepts LGBTQ people, but only about 45% of the liberal churches do, unfortunately. The debate goes on, the arguments continue. But even in the Catholic Church, priests will often tell people being homosexual may not be the problem you think it is. The official line is still the same, it says you have to live in the closet. To live in the closet is the most unhelpful state that the Church can advise anyone into. The hypocrisy in the Christian community, especially in my country, with fundamentalists and evangelicals . . . there have been clergy arrested for all kinds of crimes. I see young people today consider themselves spiritual but not religious and I understand that. I remind people over and over again, don't be a phony Christian. When you go down that path of telling lies, when you call homosexuality a sin while you're having a homosexual affair, I don't have time for you.

I would tell any young person that God loves you. It's in the scripture that Jesus knew you in your mother's womb. If God knew me in my mother's womb, then God knew who I was going to be as an adult. Coming out and finding yourself is one of the most marvelous things that can happen to you. It's like being born again. You come to terms with the fact that God really loves you, you can stay in your Church and you can make a difference there. But you've got to speak up and speak out, not let them define you but you define who you are: as a gay person and someone who is a Christian. And I say to transgender people, be yourself. Again, don't let others define you. I am so upset with our government I don't know what to do. Our crazy President says transgender people cannot serve in the military—they are already in the military. What are people frightened of? That says a lot about them.

We have just celebrated the fiftieth anniversary of my founding of the Metropolitan Community Church. I look at it and I shake my head. We were able to accomplish so much in such little time. I founded the church when I was 28 years old. Today, we are in 37 countries. Much has changed—or had up until this President . . . I look at our Church I am very thankful that I have lived.

Opposite: Reverend Troy Perry marries a gay couple, 1972. He started the Metropolitan Community Church in 1968, which welcomed and ordained LGBTQ people, as well as anybody else who wanted to attend.

"COMING OUT AND FINDING YOURSELF IS ONE OF THE
MOST MARVELOUS THINGS THAT CAN HAPPEN TO YOU.
IT'S LIKE BEING BORN AGAIN."

REVEREND TROY PERRY

PROUD
TO SERVE

Many countries ban or banned LGBTQ people from serving in their military.

This damages the armed forces and destroys lives. Keith Biddlecombe told *Attitude* magazine in 2017 about how, when he was a 20-year-old member of the Royal Navy in 1956, he was sent to military prison in Malta after being found in bed with another man. Under duress, he told the authorities about another serviceman he'd had sex with—who, on arrest, shot himself dead.

In the UK, there was much hand-wringing by the media and older high-ranking military spokespeople when activists campaigned for a change in law to accept LGBTQ personnel. Ten years after implementation (in 1999 for 2000), there was widespread acknowledgment that the change had caused no problems. Today British LGBTQ forces members march in, and recruit at, Pride parades, and new recruits are taught diversity and encouraged not to hide who they are.

In 1975, Technical Sergeant Leonard Matlovich, who was awarded the Purple Heart for service in Vietnam, attempted to sue the Air Force after he came out and was discharged. He eventually took a settlement, concluding the lawsuit, but his case saw him on the cover of *Time* magazine, making him one of the most famous gay men in America and putting the issue on the national agenda. He died from AIDS-related illnesses in 1988.

African American gay man Perry Watkins was drafted into the US military in 1967–68, despite openly acknowledging his sexuality. Still making no secret of his sexuality, he reapplied. "Every time they would open my file," he later said, "it would say 'this man is a homosexual, but he functions in an exemplary manner.'" It wasn't until 1981 when, then a Sergeant, Perry's security clearance was removed. After taking the US government to court, he was allowed to re-enlist and serve until 1984. He continued his legal battle, and in 1988 a court ruled against his treatment— the first time a US court had ruled against the military's ban on gay and lesbian service members. Perry received a promotion, back pay, a full pension, and an honorable discharge, as he chose not to re-enlist. He later stated that he felt erased from the fight against the military ban because he was Black, open about sexual behavior, and sometimes performed in drag. Perry died of AIDS-related illnesses in 1996, aged 47. Although the decision in Perry's favor was historic, progress in military policy was slow.

Above left: US Army training guide on the homosexual conduct policy, issued by the Pentagon to military personnel in 2001.

Above right: Campaign for Homosexual Equality poster, c.1976.

Opposite: Perry Watkins took the US military to court over the ban against gay and lesbian service members.

In 1993, US President Bill Clinton, who had pledged to stop gays and lesbians from being discharged, faced huge opposition and eventually compromised with the "Don't ask, don't tell" policy. It meant that serving members of the military would no longer be discharged simply for having gay sex—but only if they kept it hidden. This meant that no openly gay person could be admitted or serve in the armed forces, as it would "create an unacceptable risk to the high standards of morale, good order and discipline, and unit cohesion that are the essence of military capability."

Momentarily seen as a positive step forward, DADT was the focus of a further two decades of intense campaigning.

Lieutenant Daniel Choi served in the Iraq War as an infantry officer and then in the New York Army National Guard. In protest at DADT, he came out on *The Rachel Maddow Show* in 2009 and was discharged from the army. He began an intense campaign of chaining himself to the White House gates and of hunger strikes, and became a symbol of the campaign against "Don't ask, don't tell."

Repealing DADT in 2011, President Obama said, "As of today, patriotic Americans in uniform will no longer have to lie about who they are in order to serve the country they love . . . our armed forces will no longer lose the extraordinary skills and combat experience of so many gay and lesbian service members." More than 14,500 U.S. service members lost their jobs during the period DADT was in place.

In 2017, President Trump caused international outrage when he said that he would ban transgender people from serving in the United States military. In 2018, facing judicial pushback, the White House indicated that serving members would not be discharged, but must serve according to their "gender at birth," giving the Pentagon some discretion. As of April 2019, the administration's ban against trans individuals enlisting and serving, with the aforementioned discretion, went into effect.

Countries that allow lesbian, gay, and bisexual people to serve in their military as of 2019
(those that allow trans service personnel marked with T)

Albania	Finland (T)	Poland
Argentina	France (T)	Portugal
Australia (T)	Germany (T)	Romania
Austria (T)	Greece	Russia
Bahamas	Republic of Ireland (T)	San Marino
Belgium (T)	Israel (T)	Serbia
Bermuda	Italy	Singapore
Bolivia (T)	Japan	Slovenia
Brazil	Lithuania	South Africa
Bulgaria	Luxembourg	Spain (T)
Canada (T)	Malta	Sweden (T)
Chile	Netherlands (T)	Switzerland
Colombia	New Zealand (T)	Taiwan
Croatia	North Korea	Thailand
Czech Republic (T)	Norway (T)	UK (T)
Denmark (T)	Peru	US
Estonia (T)	Philippines	Uruguay

Above: Smiles all round as President Barack Obama repeals DADT in September 2011.

Opposite: Daniel Choi served with the US Army in Iraq in 2006–07. He came out on *The Rachel Maddow Show* in 2009, protesting DADT.

MARRIAGE

In 1970, the year after Stonewall, American students Richard Baker and James Michael McConnell took the clerk of Hennepin County, Minnesota, to court for refusing them a marriage license because they were both men. The court ruled against them and two years later, the Supreme Court of Minnesota upheld the ruling. The fight for same-sex marriage had begun.

The Netherlands made one of the first advances in 1979, when they began an "unregistered cohabitation" system, the first time anywhere in the world gave same-sex couples any meager rights. In 1984 in Berkley, California, Leland Traiman and Tom Brougham passed a new policy for city employees, coining the term "domestic partner" for the first time, and in 1985, West Hollywood created a partnership register, the first US city to do so.

In 1996, a piece of homophobic legislation that defined marriage as between a man and a woman called The Defense of Marriage Act, known as DOMA, was enacted by then-president Bill Clinton.

Some countries such as France and Germany did offer legal protections. In 1999 France began its PACS system for partners of the same sex, and in Germany, gay couples could gain partnership rights almost the same as those given to married straight people—but not quite—from 2001.

Above: Thousands gathered at Sydney Town Hall, Australia, in 2017, in support of the government's proposed postal ballot survey. The ballots asked the public: "Should the law be changed to allow same-sex couples to marry?" 61.6% voted Yes.

Opposite: Edith Windsor succeeds in her part in getting the US Supreme court to overturn Section 3 of the Defense of Marriage Act, 2013.

That same year, the Netherlands became the first country in the world to legalize same-sex marriage. Belgium was next in 2003, Spain was third and Canada fourth, both in 2005, and South Africa fifth in 2006.

In the UK, after the Blair government began scrapping homophobic laws at the turn of the millennium, it seemed activists were on a roll. It had become fashionable to demean same-sex marriage as a luxury, but in reality, the lack of partnership rights was devastating. Horrific scenarios such as women being turfed out of homes they'd shared for 30 years after the death of a partner, or men being barred from dying partners' hospital rooms after a road crash, were common.

Then, the Civil Partnership Act 2004 was voted into law. The first ceremony took place, movingly, in early December 2005 between Christopher Cramp and his partner Matthew Roche, who was suffering from cancer and died a day later. They had received special permission to become partners under the law. Marriages in Northern Ireland and Scotland followed, and on December 21, 2005, all English and Welsh couples were able to enter into civil partnerships, and pictures of Sir Elton John and David Furnish's celebration flashed across the world.

In France, Socialist Party leader Francois Hollande promised in 2004 that his party would work towards making same-sex marriage legal and, having made it an issue in his 2012 election campaign, he kept his word after becoming president. Same-sex marriage became legal in France in 2013.

Five years after civil partnerships had been legalized in the UK, Peter Tatchell's 2010 Equal Love campaign demanded marriage. The prime minister at the time, David Cameron, who had appeared on the cover of *Attitude*, was keen to support the campaign as a marker that his party had modernized. His intention was met with significant criticism from within his party and also from some gay people (the charity Stonewall did not immediately voice their support for gay marriage). But after a fight, same-sex marriage became legal in England, Scotland, and Wales, with the first marriages taking place on March 29, 2014.

Across the pond, an incredible recent hero of the LGBTQ movement stepped forward in the shape of 83-year-old Edie Windsor. Edie had been with her partner Thea Spyer for more than 40 years. They'd registered a New York-based domestic partnership in 1993 and married in Canada in 2007. When Thea died in 2009, Edie was forced to pay an inheritance tax bill of $363,053—that she wouldn't have had to pay if the US had recognized same-sex marriage. In 2010 she sued the US government for a refund and, in 2012, won.

The following year, the US Supreme Court ruled that DOMA was unconstitutional, effectively paving the way for same-sex marriage. On 26 June 2015, the eve of Pride, the Supreme Court looked back more than 50 years and overturned the ruling in the original case brought by gay student Richard Baker in 1972, legalizing same-sex marriage in all 50 states of the USA. Rapturous crowds ran to the Stonewall Inn, the scene of such pivotal change five decades before, and danced, sang, and cried throughout the night.

The momentum for marriage continued to build across the world. Germany, too, had life partnerships from 2001, and in 2017, voted for marriage. Chancellor Angela Merkel, however, voted against, saying she believed marriage meant the union "between husband and wife."

Ireland announced it would hold a referendum on the issue. In May 2015, there were emotional scenes, as Irish people across the world flew

Countries that allow same-sex marriage (as of December 2019)

Argentina	France	Norway
Australia	Germany	Portugal
Austria	Greenland	South Africa
Belgium	Iceland	Spain
Brazil	Ireland	Sweden
Canada	Luxembourg	Taiwan
Colombia	Malta	UK
Denmark	Mexico	US
Ecuador	Netherlands	Uruguay
Finland	New Zealand	

home to vote. Moving, intergenerational conversations about sexuality were had between children, parents, and grandparents for the first time, many of them broadcast on YouTube. On May 23, the result was announced. Of the eligible Irish public, 60.5% had turned out, with a result of 62% in favor of same-sex marriage and 38% against. The people of Ireland made history as the first citizens in the world to vote in same-sex marriage. The following month, 20,000 campaigners marched in Belfast to demand marriage equality in Northern Ireland—where same-sex marriage is yet to be legalized.

In August 2017, just two decades after Tasmania had finally decriminalized sex between men, Australian Prime Minister Malcolm Turnbull announced that the country would hold a plebiscite on the issue of equal marriage. The announcement unleashed waves of both excitement and opposition. Australia, which had developed a reputation for throwing one of the biggest LGBTQ parties in the world with Sydney Gay and Lesbian Mardi Gras, also has a tradition of social conservatism, and the plebiscite brought deep divisions to the surface.

Former Prime Minister Tony Abbott (who had opposed the reform despite having a lesbian sister) was headbutted during the voting period, by someone who said they did so because he "didn't think I'd get the opportunity again."

The head of Qantas, one of many national businesses to publicly support reform, had a lemon meringue pie thrown in his face by a Christian protester, and some people claimed to have felt intimidated at work due to their voting intentions.

In the event, on November 14, 2017, the results showed that more than 61.6% of all respondents (in a huge turnout of 79.5%) supported same-sex marriage. The Marriage Amendment (Definition and Religious Freedoms) Act 2017 moved through parliament on December 7, 2017, and became law two days later. The first marriages took place on December 15, 2017.

Opposite top left: Bode Mende and Karl Kreile sign their marriage certificate and become Germany's first gay couple to be legally married, in Berlin, 2017.

Opposite top right: Dutch same-sex couples cut the wedding cake after being married by Amsterdam's Mayor Job Cohen, 2001.

Opposite below: Celebration as Ireland votes in favor of same-sex marriage in a referendum, Dublin, 2015. Ireland became the first country to approve gay marriage by popular vote—62.3% voted Yes.

Top: Crowds gather on San Francisco's Castro Street, the day after the US Supreme Court ruled that same-sex couples have a constitutional right to marry nationwide, 2015.

Above: French Canadians demonstrate in front of the French Consulate in Montreal, ahead of the passing of same-sex marriage legislation in France in 2013. One sign at the event said: "Married in Quebec, single in France! Let's put an end to these contradictions."

Opposite: A couple kiss outside Argentina's congress, during a rally ahead of a senate vote to legalize same-sex marriage. In 2010, Argentina became the first Latin American country to allow gay marriage.

CULTURE: SPORTS

Drenched in machismo and sponsorship money, the world of professional sports has lagged behind in terms of LGBTQ representation. Some sports-people, such as Welsh rugby player Gareth Thomas, say they grew up feeling unable to reconcile their sexuality with their love of sport, while others have felt unable to speak out about their sexuality at all because of the threat of losing lucrative sponsorship deals or support of fans.

One of the first American professional sports-people to come out was Major League Baseball player Glenn Burke, who played for the Los Angeles Dodgers and Oakland Athletics from 1976 to 1979. Although he was out to his teammates, Dodgers management offered him $75,000 to marry a woman, which Burke refused. He left the game aged 27, saying that "prejudice won out," and died of AIDS-related illnesses in 1995.

In 1981, superstar tennis player Billie Jean King was outed when a woman she'd had an affair with sued for "palimony." She lost more than $2 million in sponsorship but went on to become one of the most high-profile sports-people in the world. When asked recently by NBC if, looking back, she would do anything differently, King responded, "I'd come out earlier." Considered by many as the best tennis player of all time, Czech-born Martina Navratilova came out in a 1981 interview and managed to rise above the steady homophobia she endured.

In the UK, the first British professional soccer player to come out was Justin Fashanu in 1990. The response was bullying, homophobic chants, and a lack of support from the soccer community, including his brother John, who infamously stated at the time that he would "not want to play or even get changed" in the same space as his brother. Justin killed himself in 1998, and his story has hung like a cloud over soccer ever since. In 2014, a year after retiring, former Aston Villa and Germany midfielder Thomas Hitzlsperger came out, and many in the FA Women's Super League are out, including former England captain Casey Stoney—but as this book goes to print, there are no openly gay soccer players in the Premier League.

Above left: Glenn Burke was the first Major League Baseball player to come out as gay. He played for the Los Angeles Dodgers and Oakland Athletics from 1976 to 1979.

Above right: Justin Fashanu, the first British professional soccer player to come out. Hounded by the press and soccer world, he took his own life in May 1998, at the age of 37.

Opposite: Martina Navratilova. Considered by many to be one of the world's greatest tennis players, Martina came out in 1981 in a newspaper interview and faced decades of homophobia. In the face of this, she won 18 Grand Slam singles titles, 31 major women's titles, and 10 major mixed titles.

Australia's Ian Roberts was the world's first rugby league player to come out, in 1995. In the UK, Welsh rugby union player Gareth Thomas came out in 2009, and Keegan Hirst became the first British rugby league player to come out in 2015.

Described as the greatest diver of all time, Olympic great Greg Louganis came out as gay in 1994 and as HIV-positive the year after. In 2008, the year he won gold at the Olympics, Australian diver Matthew Mitcham came out, and in 2013 British diver and national sweetheart Tom Daley did so too, becoming half of one of the world's most high-profile gay couples when he married screenwriter Dustin Lance Black in 2017.

John Amaechi became the first NBA player to come out in 2007, after he retired from the sport. In 2012, retired American football player Wade Davis came out. Basketball player Jason Collins came out mid-career in 2013, followed by Michael Sam in 2014 before his NFL draft.

Attitudes in the world of sports do seem to be changing. Sir David Lee Pearson is out and an 11-time gold-winning Paralympic equestrian, superstar and trans woman Caitlyn Jenner is a former Olympic gold medal-winning decathlete, and the Rio Olympics 2016 saw more out athletes than ever before: *Outsports* magazine reported a record 56 out LGBTQ athletes, with more probably unconfirmed. At the 2018 Winter Olympics, freestyle skier Gus Kenworthy and ice-skater Adam Rippon became household names in the USA. On the opening day, Kenworthy posted photos of himself with Rippon on social media, with the caption, "We're here. We're queer. Get used to it."

Above left: Italian professional volleyball player Paola Ogechi Egonu at the 2018 FIVB Volleyball Women's Nations League. From 2017 to 2018 she had a public relationship with her AGIL Volleyball teammate Katarzyna Skorupa.

Above right: Puerto Rican professional boxer Orlando Cruz, who was undefeated until 2009. He came out in 2012 while still boxing, and was among the first people to be inducted into the National Gay and Lesbian Sports Hall of Fame.

Opposite: Adam Rippon, American figure skater, won Bronze at the 2018 Winter Olympics. He's sitting on the shoulders of Gus Kenworthy, a British-born American freestyle skier, who won silver in the Men's Slopestyle at the Winter Olympics 2014. Both are out.

HATE

Hatred against LGBTQ people is sadly something that many of us across the world experience. For some it is a daily, deadly threat. Most violence against LGBTQ people is not significantly reported by the media, but more extreme events are.

In 1999, the UK suffered one of its most deadly homophobic attacks. On Saturday, April 17, a bomb exploded in the Brixton area of south London, home to a significant number of Black Londoners. Street traders had become suspicious after a man had been acting strangely and deposited a sports bag on the street in Electric Avenue. After he abandoned it, they moved it, discussing what should be done. The police were arriving as the bag, made up of fireworks and nails, detonated, injuring more than 40 people and leaving a baby, who thankfully survived, with a nail in the head. The next Saturday, another bomb inside a sports bag was left in Hanbury Street, an area home to many Asian people. Again, an onlooker became suspicious and took it to the police station, which was closed. It was in the trunk of his car when it exploded. Thirteen people were injured.

Police appealed for help and warnings were given that someone might be targeting minority groups, warning that it was possible that the gay community might be targeted.

On the evening of Friday, April 30, 1999, Old Compton Street was busy with people enjoying drinks at the beginning of the Bank Holiday weekend. Inside the Admiral Duncan pub, a quiet and unassuming gay bar, one of the oldest in Soho's gay district, a punter noticed an abandoned sports bag and told bar staff of his concerns. As manager Mark Taylor went to investigate, it exploded. The bomb caused devastation, killing three people, ripping limbs off, blinding several, and causing horrific injuries. Nick Moore, 31, John Light, 32, and Andrea Dykes, 27, three friends meeting to celebrate Andrea's pregnancy, were killed. Her husband Julian was seriously injured.

That night, 22-year-old David Copeland was arrested at his home in Hampshire, which he had turned into a far-right shrine, plastered with Nazi flags and articles about right-wing violence. Diagnosed as a paranoid schizophrenic, Copeland was convicted of murder on June 30, 2000, and sentenced to serve at least 50 years in prison.

Today there is a memorial on the ceiling of the Admiral Duncan commemorating Nick Moore, John Light, and Andrea Dykes.

At 2:09 a.m. on the morning of Sunday, June 12, 2016, the Facebook page of a small nightclub in Orlando, Florida, was updated with the message "Everyone get out of Pulse and keep running."

In the minutes before, a man had walked into the popular gay venue and spoken briefly to the security guard, before moving past him and open firing on the approximately 320 people who were finishing their Saturday night out. The security guard, an off-duty policeman, began shooting back and frantically called for police backup, which arrived as the shooter continued his spree deeper into the club, taking hostages. For three hours people cowered in toilet stalls and anywhere else they could hide, before the authorities smashed a vehicle through a toilet wall and shot the perpetrator dead. By 5:17 a.m. when the police announced that the gunman had been killed, 49 other people were dead or dying, and 53 more were injured. Until the Las Vegas concert attack of October 2017, the Pulse nightclub massacre was the most deadly single act of mass shooting by a single shooter in peacetime in United States history.

The horror of the unthinkable reverberated around the globe. A silent vigil was held outside the Stonewall Inn in New York, the Eiffel Tower and Sydney Harbor Bridge were lit up in the colors of the rainbow, and in London's Soho the leader of the Labor party, the Mayor of London, and other politicians joined the thousands who defiantly chanted, "We're here, we're queer, we will not live in fear."

Pulse had opened in 2004 in honor of one of the owner's brothers who had died of AIDS in 1991, with the intention of keeping his "pulse" alive. The evening of the attack was Latino Night, when people who may have experienced racism in the wider gay scene could go to be with friends and to feel safe. Most of the victims were in their 20s and 30s, young people on a night out, drinking, dancing, taking selfies. The attack was all the more devastating because of its location, shattering the faith that gay clubs are places of sanctuary where we are able to express our true selves

Opposite: Moments after the nail bombing of the Admiral Duncan pub on April 30, 1999, the first casualties emerge dazed.

Above: A poster of the 49 Pulse victims. Pulse was founded by Barbara Poma and Ron Legler. Poma's brother John died of AIDS in 1991, and his sister founded the venue in his memory, both as a club and as a community hub.

away from hostility. As one patron, Angel Santiago, said, "being a gay man going to a club like Pulse, it's kind of like a safe haven."

This was both the most deadly terrorist incident in the US since 9/11 and the most deadly act of violence against LGBTQ people in the history of America. Pulse's owner, Barbara Poma, has since announced her intention to create a memorial and museum on the site of the nightclub.

But unfortunately, Pulse was not the first major incident of mass violence against LGBTQ people in the US. On November 18, 1980, two gay bars in West Greenwich Village—the Ramrod and its neighboring club, Sneakers—were attacked by Ronald K. Crumpley. The former Transit Authority police officer fired 40 rounds from two handguns and a semiautomatic rifle, killing the Ramrod's doorman, 21-year-old Jörg Wenz, and a church organist from Minnesota, 32-year-old Vernon Kroening. Six others were wounded, included Rene Malute, 23, who later died of his wounds. Crumpley testified that he was having delusions that gays were servants of the devil trying to steal his soul; he was found not responsible by reason of insanity, and was committed to the Kirby Forensic Psychiatric Center, a maximum-security facility. On February 21, 1997, a lesbian nightclub in Atlanta, the Otherside Lounge, was bombed by Eric Rudolph (also known as the Olympic Park Bomber) who considered homosexuality an "aberrant lifestyle." Five patrons were injured; Rudolph was subsequently tried and convicted, and sentenced to five consecutive life terms for his serial bombings.

While there are no shortage of notable mass-casualty hate crimes toward LGBTQ people, there are even more incidents involving lone individuals targeted because of their sexual orientation or gender. Black trans women in particular experience a combination of racism, sexism,

and transmisogyny, and are targeted in hate crimes at a higher rate than any other LGBTQ persons. That's part of why Black trans women have an average life expectancy of just 27 years, and trans women overall have a life expectancy of 35. Trans women are 4.3 times more likely to be killed than all women, and at a rate seven times higher than the US national murder rate overall (1 in 2,600 vs 1 in 19,000). And the statistics for trans women of color are even worse. As of the 2019 Transgender Day of Remembrance, 85% of all trans women victims in the US that same year have been Native American trans women and/or trans women of color.

Progress continues to be slow at times in the struggle for LGBTQ legal protections, even in the face of these violent hate crimes. The "gay panic" or "trans panic" defense—a claim that unwanted sexual advances from someone LGBTQ were so distressing that the defendant was forced to assault or kill the victim in a fit of temporary insanity—continues to be employed in many places worldwide, including the UK and Australia. In the United States, where marriage equality has been a nationally-mandated right, the LGBTQ panic defense has been used much more recently than most people realize—including the murder of Daniel Spencer, a gay man in Austin, Texas, whose murderer was sentenced to a mere six months in prison in April 2018.

Above: Mourners gather in downtown Orlando to lay flowers and stage a candlelit vigil for victims of the Pulse nightclub massacre, which was, at the time, the deadliest gun attack in American history.

Opposite: Matthew Shepard was brutally attacked on October 6, 1998, and died on October 12, in a hate crime that shocked America and led to new hate crime legislation.

Overleaf: Pride events are not everyday occurrences for many around the world. Here, a woman is dragged away by police when the LGBTQ community in Istanbul attempted their own parade in 2017.

JUDY SHEPARD
MOTHER OF MATTHEW SHEPARD WHO WAS MURDERED IN A
HOMOPHOBIC HATE CRIME THAT SHOOK AMERICA IN 1998,
CO-FOUNDER OF THE MATTHEW SHEPARD FOUNDATION

My son, Matt, was a lovely, kind and compassionate young man. You may think, "Of course she would say that, she's his mum," which is true. But I'm not the only one who knows that. Even after examining all the things about him that were very annoying—and there were many—at his core, he cared. That is all he expected from other human beings—that they would care. He sought to see the best in everyone he met. He didn't think anyone was unworthy or wanted anything from him other than to be a friend.

When folks ask me, "Why would he leave the bar that night with two complete strangers, even if they did present themselves as gay to gain Matt's trust?" There are two answers to that question. One is, it was Laramie—a small college town where everyone accepts rides from anyone to get back to campus or wherever they lived. The second answer is, Matt trusted everyone. There was no such thing as a stranger to him, only potential friends. I used to think it was one of his best qualities—I wish he hadn't been so trusting that fateful night in October 1998.

How could he have possibly known the true intentions of the two young men who approached him that night pretending to be gay? How could he have known they had singled him out as vulnerable because they perceived him to be gay? Should he have been suspicious? In retrospect, of course he should have been suspicious. But in real time they were potential friends. He would not have thought they meant him harm. Matt never judged anyone by how they were dressed or presented themselves. Having grown up in Wyoming, an underpopulated blue-collar state, one never assumes anything by appearances. A person can be dressed in a bespoke suit and still have nefarious intentions—a lesson we have learned only too well in today's world.

Homophobia is easily hidden from the public at large, it can be overt—but it comes in many forms. It can be as subtle as a look or frequently used epithet that is deemed harmless—for example, "That's so gay"—or as open as shouted slurs or threats of physical violence. It can be legalized discrimination, like the ability to legally fire someone or deny them public accommodation because they happen to be gay. It is even taught from the pulpit.

The real problem is that hate is learned behavior passed down from generation to generation. We aren't brought into this world knowing how to hate or love—we learn both. We learn both or either from our family environment, our school environment, our neighborhoods, mass media, and, yes, our churches. If you can learn to hate, you can also unlearn it. It is a conscious choice to hate—it is the only thing that is a choice. Being gay, lesbian, bisexual, or transgender is not a choice—you are who are.

There are many ways hate of any kind can be addressed. We can work with educators, non-discriminatory churches, and citizens of all other marginalized communities. Each can help us understand their particular concerns. However, in the end we take our cues from public figures. Local, national, and international leaders in education, politics, law enforcement, diplomacy, business, and science. It will take leaders in every quarter of our lives to set us on the road to respect, understanding and even embracing everyone in the human race, uplifting one another to achieve every possible success and fulfill our goals in life.

That was Matt's desire—his goal in life. Shouldn't it be everyone's?

ALOYSIUS SSALI
FOUNDER OF SAY IT LOUD CLUB, SUPPORTING AND CAMPAIGNING ON BEHALF OF LGBTQ REFUGEES AND ASYLUM SEEKERS IN THE UK.

At the moment it's not possible for gay people in much of Africa to come out openly and live a normal life. People are pushed in the underground, denied the right to treatment, to socialize, to have a family life. People are tortured and many are killed due to their sexual orientation. The progress is very minimal.

Religion is one of the obstacles to the liberty of LGBTQ people in Africa. The Catholic Church and the Church of England have massive power there. All the best institutions and schools are linked to the Church. The American evangelical movement, which is relatively new, arrived in the 1980s, and started preaching against LGBTQ people. The Church has done more damage than anything. Even though there is progress in the UK, in Africa the Church is still very much against the liberty of LGBTQ people.

The Church is against so many of the efforts used to prevent the HIV virus spreading—against condoms, contraception—and what do they put in place? Absolutely nothing. It affects the general public, but it is even worse for the LGBTQ community. Most of the good hospitals are linked to the Catholic Church. You cannot go to hospitals to find a leaflet about sexual health among gay people, and people live in fear even about speaking to a nurse or a doctor if they have any kind of infection, because they think, "If I explain, I might get into trouble," so they don't.

Islamic extremism and conservative Islam too, as religious platforms, are very much against the liberties of LGBTQ people—the attitude is very, very hostile. Anyone identified as a lesbian and a Muslim can face the worst consequences. There are cases of forced marriage involving teenagers of 12 or 13, and very young people dying in childbirth. Practices like these are supported by the extremist factions of most religions. There is rarely any press reporting of this kind of thing.

Above: Eswatini (formerly Swaziland) hold their first Gay Pride event in 2018. Approximately 500 people turned up to call for equality and rights in a country where homosexuality is outlawed by the monarchy.

Opposite: Ugandan gay activist Aloysius Ssali, who runs Say It Loud Club.

When people ask what can we do, I say what is important to understand is that most of these hostile countries are major benefactors of European countries. The UK is one of the major donors, but where does the money go? Most goes to defense, to the police, the same equipment that they use against people fighting for their freedoms and liberties.

There must be a way of monitoring where the money goes. They may not want to seem like they are dictating terms, but they also have a responsibility—when you donate money, you should have a say. Historically where did we get these laws about homosexuals? Mostly from the countries that colonized Africa. They have never gone back to say it was wrong. Now let's abolish these laws which have now become incorporated into African cultures and traditions. Somehow developed counties like the UK are still contributing to the suffering of LGBT people on the African continent.

Another area is how we treat those people who come to seek asylum, on grounds of sexuality, in the UK. The image at the moment is not very good. The reception is not the best. Maybe it's about training in the Home Office. I was one of the first people to claim for asylum on grounds of sexuality in the UK, but my experience was really bad and I am still trying to raise awareness about this issue.

When people come here who are running away, they have not been used to being open; they might have never discussed their sexuality with anyone because there is no platform in those African countries to do so. That is very common. Who do you talk to? You don't speak to an auntie or an uncle; you can't speak to a nurse or counselor because you don't know what their reaction will be. So people just keep quiet, and that leads to mental health issues. People are traumatized. When people come here they are expected to explain all these things to an official. They have an interview of eight hours and are asked to talk about these sensitive issues for the first time. They may be fighting for their own life, but they struggle to reveal their emotional selves because it is too big for them. They often have issues with their sexuality. The officials expect them to behave in a way a British person might behave, and there is no way. That leads to confusion and so many cases denied. If they are deported, the main fear is torture or death. There is no protection. You are sending people back into hell.

There was a Pride event in Uganda last year, but things went wrong. I believe it is not yet the right time for parades, however much I want to see it. It's too dangerous. South Africa is liberal, but the other countries still have a lot of mistreatment, discrimination, torture, just because of people's sexuality. South Africa is the only country which is liberal. It is a hope that South Africa can maybe influence the rest of the continent and maybe Asia.

In Europe we can use the platforms we have to influence African and Asian countries. The progress is slow, but that's what keeps us going. Otherwise, if we stop, then we lose the struggle. When you see the progress made in Europe, it took some time; we believe in Africa, it might take even longer. But, as new leaders come, young people grow up, hopefully it will change.

Left: LGBTQ activists attend Uganda's first Gay Pride parade in 2012, which took place the day after Hillary Clinton hailed African LGBTQ activists as an inspiration to others worldwide.

NO ONE
LEFT BEHIND

Fifty years ago, a group of people—black, white, brown, Hispanic, street kids, young, old, drag queens, lesbians, butch lesbians, gay men, flamingly camp gay men, trans people, and those who, though we did not have the terms to describe them, would be non-binary, and more besides—said enough was enough and fought back. They put fire under the kindling of a movement that had been smoldering for the preceding decades but had not yet reached a focal point. Overnight, the actions of the Stonewall regulars and natives of New York City created an explosion of optimism and energy that sent such a bright flare high above Greenwich Village, it became a beacon for people all over the world.

The Stonewall Riots were a signal that a tipping point had arrived. Enough people had come to believe that what was happening was not okay, and that they deserved and demanded to be treated the same as everyone else. They showed that when people come together, the world can change. With organization, tenacity, time and energy, and sadly very real sacrifice, LGBTQ people across the planet did create change that those at the Stonewall Inn in 1969 could not have imagined would be possible.

It's true to say that, for most of us in the most liberal countries, our lives are unrecognizable from those that people like us had been able to live pre-1969. It is absolutely right that we should celebrate those changes and, more importantly, those who put themselves on the line so that we could all live better lives. It's hard to put into words what the tireless actions of so many people have done for our lives. There's no doubt that, as activist Peter Tatchell has said, the evolution of gay rights is one of the most successful social justice movements in history. We have gone from outlaws to in-laws within less than 50 years.

But we still live with many challenges and injustices, incredible inequalities that urgently need to be addressed. And there are new problems facing us that did not face people then, that may not be specific to LGBTQ people, but nevertheless pose threats as big as any faced in the past.

Racial inequality is a key problem for the LGBTQ community, as it is for all society. The stark reality is that LGBTQ people of color have poorer life expectations than their white counterparts. In 2016, the American Center for Disease Control released a shocking report estimating that, over their lifetimes, African American gay or bisexual men stand a 1 in 2 chance of becoming HIV-positive. For white heterosexual men it is 1 in 2,500. For the general American population it is 1 in 99, and for white gay men 1 in 11.

In other words, as things stand, half of all Black gay or bisexual men are expected to become HIV-positive in their lifetimes.

When they do become HIV-positive, African American men who have sex with men are also less likely to be able to afford the medication needed to keep them alive. In the southern states, home to about 38% of the population of America, more than 51% of all new HIV cases are diagnosed. In Mississippi and Louisiana, deaths from HIV and AIDS-related illnesses among Black gay men were seven times higher than in the rest of the population.

The figures are similarly alarming in the UK. A study in *The Lancet* in 2012 showed that in the UK, Black gay men were twice as likely to contract HIV as their white counterparts. Racism, too, is also a major problem. A survey by British magazine *FS* found that more than 80% of gay or bi men of color had experienced racism on the gay scene. It is also true that there are complicated cultural issues facing many people of color from within their communities. A BBC Asian Network survey in 2018 found significantly higher levels of homophobia among Asian people than in the general population. This means that LGBTQ people of color sometimes face elevated levels of homophobia from their families and racism from within the LGBTQ community.

Today, we have finally begun to shine light on the often-horrific violence, injustices, and experiences that transgender people suffer. The Human Rights Campaign states that in 2017, more than 29 transgender people in America died due to fatal violence, the most ever recorded. It is likely that many victims go unrecorded, and perpetrators are often not brought to justice. The Williams Institute and the American Foundation for Suicide Prevention released figures in 2014 which stated 46% of trans men and 42% of trans women had attempted suicide, far higher than the 4.6% of the overall US population. Many other studies have shown similarly disproportionately high rates of suicide and self-harm amongst trans people. It's little wonder. Across the world, transgender people are the target of hateful and untrue press reporting. Today, trans people are seen by the media as one of the last groups they can defame and attack. In the run-up to the Trump election in 2016, the issue of access to bathrooms became a major focus in America, used as a way to demonize the Left. In the UK in 2018, the government opened a consultation into the issue of possible self-identification—suggesting making it easier for trans people to be legally acknowledged as the gender they actually are (as has been law in Ireland since 2015). The media went into overdrive,

Opposite: A new generation of LGBTQ people (benefiting from the work done over the last 50 years) is emerging: freer, more expressive, and encouraging of others to be the same. Here, Olly Alexander, frontman of band Years and Years, performs at Glastonbury Festival, June 2016.

Overleaf: In 2015, relatives of Alan Turing delivered a petition to 10 Downing Street, requesting posthumous pardons for 49,000 men persecuted for their sexuality. L-r: Turing's great-nephew Nevil Hunt, great-niece Rachel Barnes, and her son Thomas.

LEWIS OAKLEY
BISEXUAL ACTIVIST

Left: Lewis Oakley is a bisexual activist who campaigns for bisexual voices to be included in the discussions about where we go next—and, indeed, included in the wider community.

So much has changed over the last 50 years, but one area we need to focus on is the great disparity in funding and attention that different subgroups of the LGBTQ acronym receive. As a bisexual man, it's disheartening to see the lack of focus that's gone in to improving the lives of bisexuals. At present, almost 90% of bisexual men remain closeted, we have some of the worst mental health and poverty figures, and there doesn't appear to be much focus on bi-specific issues in the LGBTQ movement.

What is saddening to me as a bisexual activist is seeing how isolated the majority of bisexual people are—with most having no other bisexuals in their life to turn to for support. I receive emails from bi people all across the globe. The majority are dealing with the same issues. Bisexuality appears to be stuck in a constant state of infancy because the majority have no other bi people to turn to for advice or inspiration. How can we grow when no one around us can teach us how to handle our attractions to more than one gender? The bisexual community hasn't been able to come together and trade notes and help each other the way the gay community has.

I hope we can bring more bisexuals together so that discussions can be had, allowing us to evolve to a place where bisexuality no longer has the stigma

associated with it. I hope that future generations will be able proclaim their sexuality without fear of how it will impact their lives and, much like at Stonewall, have a community of people ready to back them up.

I don't want people to go through what I've gone through, constantly having their sexuality questioned, becoming the verbal punching bag for gay men and having female partners constantly told I'll cheat. The ignorance around bisexuality in society shocks me. Even from our own community, attitudes leave much to be desired. So many groups are happy to call themselves LGBTQ, but they are not so keen to tell you what they do specifically to support bisexuals, and it's beyond time the B stops falling through the cracks.

While my goal is to focus on strengthening the bisexual arm of the LGBTQ community, I have great hopes for the overall movement. As we look towards the next 50 years, I hope for a day when sexuality comes with no social stigma. A day when all disparities have been corrected. A day when sexuality has no implications on a person's mental health, likelihood of poverty, and all the other areas in which we know there are problems.

obsessively suggesting that trans women were a threat to cisgender women. The charity Mermaids—in reality offering lifesaving support for kids and their families—was painted as a sinister organization intent on changing the gender of the nation's children. In early 2019, local papers reported the murder of Amy Griffiths, 51, a much-loved trans woman from Worcester, England. Paris Lees pointed out that if it had been Amy who had murdered someone, her face would have been on the cover of national newspapers and used to portray trans people as perpetrators of violence, rather than the reality that so often they are victims of it. Weeks later, the media reported the extremely grisly murder in Brazil of Quelly da Silva, a 35-year-old trans woman. It seems violence against transgender people continues to be ignored.

Intersectionality is a term which simply expresses the fact that people are not just "one thing," or affected by one issue. So, for instance, a low-income, black trans woman might be affected by sexism, racism, transphobia, and economic hardship. A white, working-class gay man might suffer from homophobia and issues around low income, among others. Lesbians have long been subject to both homophobia and sexism. The policing of both women's behavior and the way women present themselves is still a problem in our society, and one that seems to be used against lesbians particularly powerfully. It's right that we should not be defined by such issues, but they are crucially important to understand in the fight for wider LGBTQ rights.

One issue where "intersectional issues" come together is that of homelessness. All over the world, where statistics exist, a disproportionate number of homeless people, and especially young people, are LGBTQ. According to the Williams Institute in the US, in 2012 40% of homeless youth served by agencies identified as LGBTQ. A University of Chicago study suggests LGBT youth are 120% more likely to experience homelessness.

In the UK, the Albert Kennedy Trust states that the top three reasons service users report as causing their homelessness were parental rejection; sexual, physical and emotional abuse from within the family; and aggression and violence from within the family.

It's still true that much of the LGBTQ movement focuses more on men and less on women. We know that sexism intersects with homophobia directed towards women. Comedian Hannah Gadsby painfully addressed the issue of male violence against lesbians in her stand-up show *Nanette*, which streamed on Netflix, and has been lauded for bringing this issue to light for a mainstream audience. I would argue that many lesbians and gay men have incredibly close relationships, but gay male misogyny is not as rare as we might hope. After actor Rose McGowan suggested during a podcast discussion with writer Brett Easton Ellis that gay men were more misogynistic than straight men, there was uproar. While many gay men argued this was not the case, it is certainly true that gay culture is not always entirely respectful to womanhood. So much of gay culture centers on worshiping and adulating heightened, day-glo presentations of female glamour, but we have not always respected the basic needs and reality of real women. In many countries around the world, lesbians experience homophobia in a brutally unique way, being "correctively" raped—something that is not met with the global outrage it should be. Jamaican activist Angeline Jackson spoke out about her experiences in *Marie Claire* in 2016, of growing up with homophobic rules

left over from colonial rule, having to go to conversion therapy, and being brutally sexually assaulted as a teenager. This ordeal spurred her into co-founding advocacy group for lesbian and bisexual women, Quality of Citizenship Jamaica. She states: "I won't say it has been easy to speak out. I will say, though, that I couldn't have lived my life any other way."

Today some of the balance is beginning to be addressed, because of young people. A generation is coming of age, having grown up in the recent years of the struggle and having a stronger sense of their right to be themselves. Because of social media, young women, bi people, and those using new terms to describe themselves are able to assert their identities, often with the popular LGBTQ youth hashtags that trend regularly across the world. More and more bisexual people, and those people who are happy to admit they are bisexual or "curious," or any number of identities, are being seen. It is also heartening to see that people who are "intersex," born with sex characteristics that are not exclusively male or female, are finally coming out into the daylight, with figures such as Seven Graham, the world's first out intersex comedian, who is also producing a film on the subject.

We know that, despite the advances, every year there are news stories of LGBTQ young people taking their lives because of bullying—and sometimes having their lives taken from them by the people who should be there to protect them—because of their sexual orientation or gender identity. For example Giovanni Melton, 14, from Henderson, Nevada, was shot dead by his father Wendell Melton in 2017.

Incredibly, 17 states of America still lack LGBTQ protection laws. Sex education across the world mostly does not address the needs of LGBTQ people. In the UK, sexual health cuts disproportionately affect gay and bi men, since we have higher rates of HIV and other STIs. Worldwide, it is illegal to be gay or lesbian in 72 countries; in eight of them people can face the death penalty.

In recent years Sylvia Rivera, Marsha P. Johnson, and Stormé Delaverie have become powerful symbols of the failings of the LGBTQ movement to adequately address the issues of poverty, racism, and the needs of lesbians,

Opposite: Janet Mock is a transgender activist speaking her truth to the mainstream and being met with love and support. A bestselling author and presenter, she co-wrote, produced, and directed the hit FX show *Pose*.

Above: Benjamin Melzer broke new ground by becoming the first trans man to appear on the cover of European *Men's Health* magazine, in April 2016.

WILL YOUNG
SINGER-SONGWRITER, AND CO-PRESENTER AND
WRITER OF LGBTQ-FOCUSED PODCAST *HOMO SAPIENS*

Wellbeing and mental health are such big phrases and are so much a part of the fabric of everyday conversation nowadays. As a speaker and advocate for both of these things, I still don't feel comfortable using the word "mental" when describing our health. I suppose "mental" has a stronger affinity with instability and being crazy than it does with being normal and an everyday human.

I like to think of the mind and the body working as one. For me, I believe trauma is such a huge factor, if not the overriding factor, in our physical and mental wellbeing. It stays with us more in our bodies than our minds, and the body ultimately runs the show with our minds playing catch-up, trying to make sense of the whole thing. Our bodies get stuck in fight, flight, or freeze mode. We disassociate, turning to addictions to get us through the day. There is then a lot of shame that comes with feeling anxious or depressed, and shame is certainly something that LGBT people experience in by the bucketload. From day one, the message from the powers that be is that we are wrong, less than human, freaks. To be gay at school is the ultimate crushing accusation, it brings about segregation and social exclusion in the extreme. We feel unsafe in the world and we have to be on guard in the playground, at home, and merely walking the streets. We are afraid to show our love and our need to express who we are is crushed. Without expression, we are nothing. Our soul and spirit get destroyed—is it any wonder that LGBT people's mental health is far more at risk than that of heterosexuals? How can one exist with such deep soul-wounding? We internalize this pain and turn it onto ourselves, leading to excruciating shame and internalized homophobia against ourselves and our brothers and sisters.

The route out of this quagmire of shame hoisted upon us by society can be long and terrifying. Indeed, it can be a lifetime of work. It is, however, possible. I've walked the walk. I've done the hero's journey, the soul retrieval, the necessary processing in the mind and the body to release the trauma and feel safe and sit easy with myself. I'll always carry it with me, but I turn to the queer movement begun in the mid-1990s that focused on gay shame as a driving force behind activism and self-empowerment. Embrace the shame, use it as a motivational factor. Feel the love and compassion, don't get overtaken by rage, rather use the anger and sense of injustice to walk tall and proud. Shame can walk hand-in-hand with gay pride. Connect with your humanity and the humanity of your brothers and sisters and rejoice in who you are.

Right: Will Young won music competition series *Pop Idol* in 2002. He has since frequently spoken publicly about the mental health effects of growing up gay in a homophobic society, and covers this among other issues on his podcast *Homo Sapiens*.

Opposite top: In 2017, allegations began to emerge that LGBTQ people in Chechnya were disappearing, being rounded up, tortured, and even being murdered by the state. Protests took place across the world, pictured here is one in Madrid.

Opposite below: Activist DeRay McKesson is one of the key figures in the Black Lives Matter movement in the US, showing the importance of intersectionality and protesting issues that might not be specific to LGBTQ people but affect us all. In a 2018 interview with *Out* magazine, McKesson said, "One of the important things about being out, especially at the beginning of the protests given my platform, is that I didn't want people to think that the only way that I had a platform was by hiding."

transgender people and gender nonconforming people. These individuals may still yet come to play the most important role in our movement, since they provide a much-needed wakeup call that of equal importance to our movement are issues that may not seem specifically LGBTQ issues. Racism and poverty prematurely ended the lives of Marsha P. Johnson and Sylvia Rivera, in particular.

If we want to survive another fifty years, then we must urgently tackle the injustice of poverty, the homo- and transphobia of religion, and the inequality and injustice that fuels the rise of the far right across the world. As I have written before, the gay community thrived in Berlin in the 1930s, before economic collapse and other factors brought the rise of the far right. Global socioeconomic issues have a huge effect on the progress of equality, and the looming environmental breakdown that the climate crisis presents us with presents a challenge to the whole of society, but particularly minorities. The science of climate change is settled and, in 2018, legendary broadcaster Sir David Attenborough joined the scientific warnings, saying "the collapse of our civilizations and the extinction of much of the natural world is on the horizon." The LGBTQ movement has been largely silent about this, seemingly unable to see that if we do not stop the destabilization of our world, the rights we've fought for could evaporate before our eyes.

It is right, though, that we should celebrate the place in the journey in which we find ourselves. Since the turn of the millennium, and in particular in the last decade, so many advances have happened it is hard to quantify them.

LGBTQ representation in the media and in sports, as covered earlier in the book, is improving all the time. The demand for accurate and varied representation has seen many figures achieve stellar success in the last few years. More mainstream TV names than ever are out, with Anderson Cooper, Don Lemon, Rachel Maddow, *Good Morning America's* Robin Roberts, Sue Perkins, Alan Carr, and Simon Amstell all featuring on primetime shows. The worlds of pop music, and to a lesser extent alternative music, have their own stars—Frank Ocean, Sam Smith, King

Princess, Laura Jane Grace of Against Me!, Kele Okereke of Bloc Party, Troye Sivan, and Olly Alexander have legions of fans all over the world. Audiences and the Hollywood establishment were enthralled by 2015's *Tangerine*, 2016's *Moonlight* and 2017's *Call me by Your Name*; actors such as Ezra Miller, Cara Delevingne, Jonathan Groff, and Laverne Cox are all stars in the ascendant; and director, producer, and writer Lee Daniels deserves a special mention for his uncompromising vision of bringing the stories of LGBTQ people of color to television screens in the smash hit series *Empire*. Writer Janet Mock wrote in her memoir *Redefining Realness* (2014) about her quest for identity as a transgender woman, becoming a *New York Times* bestselling author and a twenty-first century heroine.

Though it is still a desperate problem, the rates of HIV infection have begun to fall for the first time. HIV stigma remains, but more and more people feel confident to be open about their HIV status, such as British MP Lloyd Russell-Moyle, who stood before the British House of Commons in November 2018 and described his journey to acceptance of his status.

Though there is a long way to go, due to books such as *The Velvet Rage* by Alan Downs and, I hope, my book *Straight Jacke*t, we are finally airing the painful need to address both the mental health problems that can occur as the result of growing up in cultures of shame, as well as the higher levels of addiction that result. More and more groups are being set up to help LGBTQ people deal with these issues from the "Let's Talk About Gay Sex and Drugs" discussion event in London, through to the LGBT centers in LA and New York.

Opposite: Timothée Chalamet and Armie Hammer in *Call Me By Your Name* (2017)—the film won screenwriter James Ivory an Academy Award for Best Adapted Screenplay, but has since spurred discussion on the appropriateness of casting straight, cis actors in LGBTQ roles.

Above: Jonathan Groff disproved one of Hollywood's golden rules—that audiences would not accept an out gay actor playing a heterosexual leading man—when he starred in Netflix's outstanding 2017 crime drama *Mindhunter*.

Left: The crowd celebrates as the legislation that recriminalized homosexuality in India was reversed in 2018, meaning that homosexual sex was finally legal in the country, in a landmark ruling that sent waves and joy around the world.

Below: A long way from 1969: revelers at New York Pride, 2018.

Overleaf: Young members of the Gay Liberation Front, New York, 1969, photographed by Peter Hujar. The image was used for a GLF poster urging young people to "COME OUT!" signaling a new dawn, a new energy, and a new optimism that would changes people's lives even 50 years later.

A final irony of our movement is that most of the people who struggled so hard to make it possible to be out, and the head of a tech company or a Hollywood superstar, did not get riches or fame, or sometimes even acknowledgment. There are many more people, thousands even, who played key roles in the early days of the LGBTQ movement, but whom I have not been able to include here. To all of them, we say thank you. We simply would not be here without them.

Harry Hay has been called the father of gay liberation. He conceived of an organization for gay men in 1948 and on November 11, 1950, he, his partner, and three friends held the first meeting of the Mattachine Society, then called the Society of Fools. Although now often viewed as too conservative, Harry Hay and the Mattachine Society were the first formal, organized beginnings of a fight back against gay oppression in the US. Harry died on October 24, 2002.

Craig L Rodwell is one of the most important figures in LGBTQ emancipation. He ran the Oscar Wilde Bookshop and was a one-time partner of Harvey Milk, who whipped up the press during the riots, printed leaflets, and galvanized the movement into starting the Gay Pride march. In 1992 he was honored with a special Lambda Literary Award. He died of stomach cancer on 18 June 1993 in St Vincent's Hospital, New York City, aged 52.

Frank Kameny, who co-founded the Washington, DC, branch of the Mattachine Society in 1961 with Jack Nichols, was responsible for the first American gay protests. He became the first openly gay person to run for Congress, in 1971, a race he lost but which led to the formation of the Gay and Lesbian Alliance of Washington DC. He died on October 11, 2011, at his home in Washington, DC, aged 86.

Phyllis Lyon and Del Martin were the couple responsible for starting the lesbian group The Daughters of Bilitis in 1955. They went on to fight homophobia in groups such as the National Organization for Women. They got married on June 16, 2008, after the California Supreme Court made marriage legal. Del died later that year.

Barbara Gittings is one of the key figures of the LGBTQ movement, having founded the New York branch of the lesbian group Daughters of Bilitis, edited the lesbian review *The Ladder*, and worked closely with Frank Kameny to start the first American gay protests. With Kameny she organized a meeting of the American Psychiatric Association, which lead to homosexuality being declassified as a mental illness in 1973. She met her partner Kay Tobin in 1961 and the two were together for more than 50 years. Barbara died in 2007 in Kennet Square, Pennsylvania.

The Manford family are among the most unsung heroes of the LGBTQ movement. Having been present at the Stonewall riots, teenaged Morty Manford became an activist and inspired his mother and father, Jeanne and Jules, to start what became Parents, Families, and Friends of Lesbians and Gays. Morty died of AIDS-related illnesses in 1992, aged 41. Jeanne died in 2013, aged 92, and is survived by her daughter Suzanne. In 2014, a street in Flushing, Queens, New York, was renamed Jeanne, Jules, Morty Manford PFLAG Way.

Marsha P. Johnson suffered from severe mental health problems and addiction and was arrested, in her estimation, more than 100 times. In the days after the New York Pride parade, on 6 July 1992, Marsha's body was found in the Hudson River. Her death, at the age of just 46, was ruled as suicide, but her friends have always speculated that she did not take her own life. There were reports that Marsha had been harassed by a group of men on the night she died, and that a man who had been seen fighting her had bragged about killing her. In 2012, her case was reopened by the New York Police Department.

Sylvia Rivera also suffered from mental health problems and addiction. She was homeless for much of her life, but in her later years experienced gratitude from the LGBTQ community for her key role in the Stonewall riots and the movement that followed. Sylvia attended the Metropolitan Community Church set up by Reverend Troy Perry (pages 138–39) and was passionate about distributing food to the poor and helping queer youth. The MCC's New York queer youth shelter is named Sylvia's Place. She died of complications from liver cancer at St Vincent's Hospital, New York, on February 19, 2002.

Stormé Delaverie is believed to have been the "butch" lesbian who fueled the Stonewall uprising by fighting with the police as she was bundled into the back of a police wagon, asking for help—and getting it. She remained a bouncer, performer, and defender of women, until her death in 2014, aged 93.

In his book *Stonewall*, David Carter states that it was an unnamed drag queen who first retaliated to a police officer by hitting him with her handbag, and that a Puerto Rican man known as Gino threw a cobble stone at a police car, causing the police to barricade themselves inside the bar. And the rest is, literally, history.

It is testament to Stonewall that 50 years ago you would be fired from your job for being gay, and now many of the biggest global companies in the world have very active pro-LGBTQ diversity policies intended to support their staff and make employees feel they can be themselves. It is a undoubtedly a great thing that Tim Cook, the head of one of the most prominent companies in the world, Apple, is an out gay man, but it also throws a painful irony into relief: that the people who fought hardest at Stonewall were the homeless street kids and, today, while the head of one of the most valuable businesses in history can be out, many LGBTQ people live in poverty, and cannot afford healthcare. For many African American gay and bisexual men and others this is not just a cruel irony, but something that costs them their lives.

Globally, the picture is more mixed. In many homophobic countries, as the Internet makes the global LGBTQ community more visible, it seems some governments react by becoming more draconian and hateful. Indonesia has been publicly flogging gays and lesbians before crowds, in increasing numbers. Though not illegal to be gay in Egypt, the country is believed to be doubling down on its persecution of gay people. In January 2019, Egyptian TV presenter Mohammed al-Ghiety was sentenced to one year's hard labor simply for interviewing a gay man. The same month it was reported that Iran hanged a gay man who, it said, had kidnapped two teenagers, though commentators believe that is not true. In January 2019 it was reported that Chechnya has once again begun terrorizing, kidnapping, and sometimes allegedly killing gay people. A painful thing which we often don't acknowledge is that life is still unbearable to the point of unlivable for LGBTQ people in many countries, and we need to find the courage to speak out about it more.

But there is progress, from Ireland and Australia's votes to legalize equal marriage, through to even bigger advances due to the tireless work from LGBTQ activists. Mozambique decriminalized lesbian and gay relationships in 2015. In April 2018, largely due to the work of Jason Jones, the Trinidad and Tobago High Court ruled that the criminalization of consensual sodomy was unconstitutional. In September 2018, the Indian High Court finally ruled that a British colonial-era law, which had been in force for 160 years, was also unconstitutional and struck it out. In 2019 Angola removed its anti-gay "vices against nature" provision, which had been used to persecute gay people.

Without doubt, parts of Europe are the most progressive places in the world for LGBTQ rights. Denmark decriminalized gay sex in 1933, Iceland in 1940, and Sweden in 1944. In 2001 the Netherlands was the first country in the world to legalize same-sex marriage. It was followed by Belgium and Canada. Sweden was the first country, in 1972, to legally allow citizens to undergo gender confirmation surgery and have access to free hormone therapy. European countries are usually acknowledged as the best places to be LGBTQ by polls and advocacy groups: ILGA-Europe ranked Malta, Belgium, and Luxembourgh the highest in 2019, and the Spartacus Gay Travel Index for the same year put Sweden and Portugal in top place, along with Canada. Much of western Europe has seen an incredible transformation of the experience of LGBTQ people over the last 50 years. The EU has had a positive effect on gay rights within Europe because intolerance conflicts with the EU tenet of free movement. There is recognition of same-sex unions in 22 of the 28 EU member states, same-sex marriage in 15, and 25 states have full anti-discrimination policies.

But that's not the whole story. The Rainbow Europe Annual Review for 2019 suggested intolerance was still rife in Italy, for instance. Many countries in central and eastern Europe do not have equal laws, and public attitudes can be overwhelmingly hostile. Bulgaria, in 1991, became the first country in Europe to place a constitutional ban on same-sex marriage, followed by many other eastern European countries, the most recent being Slovakia in 2014.

Turkey's President Erdoğan, widely seen as pushing a more Islamist agenda, is considered hostile to LGBTQ people. In 2019, once again, the Istanbul Gay Pride march was banned, and police used tear gas and rubber bullets to stop it. In 2017 the Pride Committee issued a statement saying, "We are not alone, we are not wrong, we have not given up." Infamously in 2013, Russia created a law prohibiting the promotion of homosexuality, despite it being legal to be gay in that country since 1993. A 2019 survey found that 47% of the Russian public were in support of LGBTQ equal rights, reflecting an increase in tolerance over the past 20 years, but the 2013 law still effectively outlaws homosexuality.

A 2018 Ipsos poll found that Canada, Sweden, and Argentina were the most trans-friendly countries in the world. But, in that same year, a shocking 14 European countries still required sterilization of trans people before their gender was legally recognized. Only 17 European states have specific policies against transphobic violence and only 26 have policies explicitly protecting trans people from discrimination. Argentina was the first country in the world to pass a law allowing gender self-identification in 2012, followed by many countries in western Europe—Denmark was the first in the region in 2014.

Despite the ongoing issues and horrific injustices that exist across the globe, incredible advances have been made too. It is astonishing to think that those people who picketed and fought and kicked and supported one another in the years before and on the night of the Stonewall riots, fueled a movement which has changed lives all over the world.

Following the riots, the Stonewall Inn was not considered the landmark that it is today. Directly afterward it was seen as a place of civil disorder and, under boycott by the local gay community because of its Mafia links, it was abandoned and soon ceased to run as a gay venue. During the 70s and 80s other businesses used it for different reasons. In the 90s it became a mainstream nightclub. In March 2007, it was reopened as a popular queer venue. Today LGBTQ people from all over the world come to the Stonewall Inn to have a drink and to have their picture taken outside the place which changed their lives. The Stonewall serves as a focal point for New York's queer community in times of triumph and tragedy. The world acknowledges it as the place where, fifty years ago, we began to find ourselves and to assert the truth. It was the place where we realized, as one anonymous person—who may have been white or black, man or woman, rich or poor, transgender or not—said during the uprising 50 years ago, "We may be different, but we are not inferior."

Since that realization, both small and enormous, we have celebrated the Stonewall riots in countries all over the world. From the families of all kinds who show their support in London every year, to the huge annual EuroPride events across the Continent, to the marches in Spain and Brazil, people continue celebrating. They carry that spirit, even in Turkey where they fight for their lives, facing water cannon and police brutality, and in Uganda where they take tentative baby steps against oppression many of us could not imagine. In those places the rainbow flag is more than just a sticker in a Starbucks shop window or an emoji; for them it remains, as it was when first adopted by the LGBTQ community, a powerful symbol of hope for a better life.

To those who continue to fight, we stand with you.

To those who fought and bled for us—female, male, everything in between; black, white, brown, Hispanic; lesbian, gay, trans, non-binary; butch or femme—we say thank you.

But more importantly, we MUST honor these people by finding the courage to overturn todays injustices, for all of us—regardless of income, gender identity, skin color or nationality—and to safeguard the future for the generations that follow us.

The fight goes on.

Over to you.